Liber des Goules

The Book of Ghouls ™

P9-AEX-995

Kevin Brown G50-9511

Credits

Written by: Glenys Ngaire McGhee

Additional Writing by: Richard E. Dansky

Development by: Richard E. Dansky, Cynthia Summers and Ken Cliffe

Editing by: Cynthia Summers and Ken Cliffe

Art Direction by: Lawrence Snelly

Interior Photography by: Niki Fridh, J. Lank Hancock & Ronni Radner

Front and Back Cover Design: Lawrence Snelly

Layout and Typesetting by: Lawrence Snelly

Models: Julian Draven, Becky Allen, Tim Kratz, Diana McCreary, Chris Mullins, Regeana Morris, Amanda Raven, Jason Vaughan, Ace Ebele, Page Gleason, Dan Edmonds, J. Michelle Jones, Rob Hatch, Larry Friedman, Diane Zamojski, Kim Pullen, Justin Achilli, Cynthia Summers, Valerie Emerick, Paul LePree, Louvie Locklear, Ian Locklear, Todd Shaughnessy, Benjamin Stuart, Rebecca Schaeffer, Michael Rollins, Laurah Norton and Richard Dansky.

The Developers would like to thank all of our playtesters. You know who you are.

Special Thanks To:

Stephe "Motel Six" **Pagel**, for leaving the light on for interns.

Cary "Occasionally We Bitch" **Goff**, for not having read **Wraith**, either.

Stewart "D. Niall" **Wieck**, for taking exception to going through shadow.

Phil "Mr. Friday Night Special" **Brucato**, for finding good press in the oddest of places.

Ethan "Space Dragullahs of Vagisil" **Skemp**, for things that I'm not allowed to share in a family roleplaying supplement.

Ronni "I Am Editor, Hear Me Roar" **Radner**, for identifying a leeeetle too closely with **Masquers**.

Dana "Rant Mistress" **Buckelew**, for keeping accurate track of that vital vitriol. (We're going to miss you.)

Greg "Buster Zoltan" **Fountain**, for doing us all proud by bringing a little bundle of joy into the world, and having the brains to stay the hell out of the office for a while when the kid arrived.

© 1997 White Wolf, Inc. All rights reserved. Reproduction without the written permission of the publisher is expressly forbidden, except for the purposes of reviews and the reproduction of blank character sheets for personal use only. White Wolf and Vampire the Masquerade are registered trademarks of White Wolf, Inc. All rights reserved. Mind's Eye Theatre, Masquerade Second Edition, Werewolf the Apocalypse, Ghouls:Fatal Addition Apocalypse, Liber des Goules, Antagonists and Laws of the Night are trademarks of White Wolf, Inc. All rights reserved. All characters, names, places and text herein are copyrighted by White Wolf, Inc.

The mention of or reference to any company or product in these pages is not a challenge to the trademark or copyright concerned.

Because of the mature themes involved, reader discretion is advised.

Check out White Wolf online at http://www.white-wolf.com; alt.games.whitewolf and rec.games.frp.storyteller

PRINTED IN CANADA.

WHITE WOLF
GAME STUDIO

Table of Contents

A Cautionary Tale: Hideaway

In love, in love with the other one,
the one who doesn't know.
And when we dance with the other one,
the eyes of fury glow!
— The Creatures, "Fury Eyes"

Compared to the stake through her breast, Lanaugha thought, the spider attempting to spin a web in her left ear was only a minor annoyance. It wouldn't have been an annoyance at all had she been able to move, but the piece of white pine messily inserted between her third and fourth ribs meant that moving was no longer an option. Of course, she reflected, the spider was definitely the least of her problems at this point.

On the other hand, if her current captivity continued much longer, the spider and its arthropod companions might well become a concern. While her dead flesh was still far too tough for the mandibles of the spiders and centipedes that swarmed the crawl space she'd been unceremoniously stuffed into, she could still feel the tickling of their feet with exquisite precision. Every footfall, every step, every sensation went straight to her too-active mind. It would probably drive her mad before long.

The time the centipede walked across her still-open left eye was the worst. She screamed, or tried to, but she couldn't even move that much. As hard as she tried, no words would come. No sound would come. And so Lanaugha was trapped in silent frenzy for those nine hours, unresponsive muscles straining against invisible bonds that wouldn't permit her so much as a whimper. It had been nine hours of

hell, made worse by the fact that when Jace came home, he immediately checked on her. He cradled her head in his hands and muttered his half-sensible endearments and apologies. He bathed her face with a cool wet cloth and told her how much he loved her. Then, when his sense of guilt was assuaged, he lowered the boards and sealed her in the dark again.

The centipedes took all of half a minute to return.

So here she was, trapped in a six-by-three-by-two hideaway in her favorite ghoul's laundry room. Never mind that she'd given Jace the money to buy the house (asking only that he make one room light-proof, just in case). Never mind that she had supported him for years (it was only right, as the work he did for her precluded his holding a normal job). Never mind that she'd given him the blood.

She should have suspected something long ago, she told herself for the thousandth time. There were so many clues, so many hints, and she ignored them all. She ignored the danger, as she had for so many years with so many other ghouls. Silently, she resolved to be much more careful the next time around.

The next time. That was a laugh. Jace was probably going to keep her down here as long as the house stood, feeding her enough thin animal blood to sustain her, but never letting her move again. And once a month he would come to worship at the altar of her bleeding wrist and love her all the more for it.

All the ghouls had loved her, and that had been part of the problem. It was accepted, really; if you had a ghoul, you Bound him, and the love inspired in him would be enough to keep him in line. Certainly there were the horror stories about ghouls who turned on their Regnants, but Lanaugha dismissed them as pure fancy, a sort of vampiric urban legend. Besides, all of those lurid anecdotes (ending with the poor innocent vampire being staked out for the sun by a horribly vengeful ghoul) had one thing in common. Inevitably, it was horrible mistreatment of the ghouls that made them strike back, tortures and abuses that Lanaugha had never so much as considered. Ghouls were just too valuable to risk damaging that way. No, she had always been extremely kind to her ghouls. Next time she would simply have to be firmer.

There was a loud clanking from above the claustrophobic crawl space. Jace was apparently dragging something heavy and metallic down the basement stair; there was a pattern of rhythmic thunks interspersed with curses. Well, there wasn't much that she could do from here, one way or the other. It wasn't as if she'd picked Jace for his brawn, anyway.

It was her kindness that led to this, Lanaugha decided. She'd been too kind to Jace, and in his infatuated state, he decided that she actually returned his affection. It was preposterous, of course — he'd been her ghoul for almost 10 years and the perfect Servitor throughout that time. Every assignment had been completed with style and efficiency, and she appreciated his work. That was why she bought him the house. The parameters of the relationship were clear and under- stood.

At least, that was what she thought. Obviously, she'd been wrong. But what was the turning point?

She could think of two possibilities. The first occurred nearly three years ago. He'd finished performing some task or other — at this point she could hardly remember what it had been, something to do with a judge — and she made the mistake of smiling at him for a little too long, and of calling him her "dearest Jace."

It was just a figure of speech, but she felt his eyes on her back the rest of that night. Jace had never watched her that way before, not with that predatory intensity. Like an idiot, she attributed it to the Bond and thought no more of it, even though he watched her that way more and more over the nights that followed.

She never called him "dearest" again, but it was plain that Jace hungered to hear it. She remembered thinking something to herself about not encouraging him, and then of not giving the matter any more thought.

Damn, the mistakes were mounting. She would have smiled, were she able to.

Then the floorboards were pulled away, and her eyes were flooded with harsh fluorescent light.

Jace was there, of course, his face a mask of tender concern. In his left hand was what could only be a carafe full of blood. In his right was, incongruously, a turkey baster. "And how is my beautiful Lanaugha this evening?" he cooed, dropping oh so slowly to his knees so as to not spill the blood, and planted a soft kiss on her forehead. "I have some good news and some bad news. Which do you want to hear first?"

Expertly, he dipped the baster into the blood and drew forth a generous helping, and then slid the nozzle between Lanaugha's lips. He pressed gently on the bulb, making the precious vitae trickle into her system. With a shock, she realized that the blood Jace was feeding her was human. While she didn't mind the extra strength it gave her, not to mention the much more satisfying taste, in three months of captivity Jace had never, ever fed her human blood. Why now?

"Well, I see you've discovered the good news. Yes, this is from a human. You've been such a good girl, I thought you deserved a treat. Don't worry, I checked to make sure there were no nasty drugs or diseases. It took me a while, you know. You could at least say thank you." He filled the baster and inserted it again. "Ah, well, I'm sure you would thank me if you could." Much too slowly, the blood leaked down, spreading its delicious warmth. Eventually, the nozzle emptied and Jace paused to refill it.

"There is bad news, you know. Your friend Drake has been asking questions about your whereabouts. He seems to think I had something to do with it, and has even insinuated that I've hurt you somehow. That shows you how silly Drake is. You know I'd never do anything to hurt you."

You put a goddamned stake in my heart and locked me in a box with the termites for three months, you bastard! she wanted to scream, but her lips would not so much as twitch. Instead, the baster, full of warm sweet blood, was placed between her teeth again. To be fed thus, like a baby, was humiliating. If she ever got free, Jace was going to pay.

Eventually, inevitably, the blood ran out. Jace planted a single kiss on her cold lips, then stood. Oddly enough, he didn't replace the floorboards. "I've got a little something to take care of, love, then I'll be right back. Don't go anywhere." Then he was gone, out of her field of vision, and she could hear his footfalls ascending the basement stairs. Off in the corner of the room, she could see some sort of tank. That must have been what Jace lugged down, but for the life of her Lanaugha couldn't figure out what it might be for.

Still, Jace was gone, and that gave her time to return to her original train of thought. The other thing that might have triggered Jace occurred when she took Paul on as a ghoul. Paul was a lawyer, and a rather handsome one at that. She met him at a party on a Saturday and Bound him to her by the following Wednesday.

Alone among her ghouls, Jace did not seemed thrilled with the addition. At the time, he had been the newest, and it was always natural for the "youngest" to resent a new arrival. Jace had been resented by Carpenter, the ghoul she'd taken just before. Then again, Carpenter's dislike faded with the years, while Jace's crystallized into an icy hatred.

Come to think of it, it was after Paul's addition to her staff that the accidents started to happen. Carpenter was killed by a hit-and-run driver; Jace delivered the news as quickly as he could, but she got there just a little too late. Six months later, Paul was executed by the prince for a breach of the Masquerade. His Majesty the Most Asinine Prince Vincent didn't mention where he got the evidence that Paul had shot his mouth off, but it was effectively damning. And every time another ghoul disappeared, Jace convinced her not to create a replacement, that he could do the work of all.

He instead made her more reliant on him, she now saw. By the time Jace staked her, he was her only ghoul. Apparently that wasn't enough, though. He was still afraid that she might take another. That he might have competition. That it wouldn't be just the two of them forever.

There was the sound of an argument upstairs, then the slamming of a door. She heard Jace's feet on the stairs again, and more cursing. She could vaguely see him come into the room and start fiddling with the metal tank he'd hauled down earlier. There was a low hiss, and Lanaugha was suddenly afraid.

When should she have known? When Jace said that he'd created the safest hiding place imaginable for her, and begged her to come look at it? When the last of her other ghouls disappeared? When Drake warned her about things that Jace had said to his ghouls? She'd been a fool.

Jace was back. He looked worried. There was something small and silvery in his left hand. "I'm sorry I had to go, love," he apologized. Distantly, she could hear someone pounding on the front door. "That was Drake again. He claims to know what happened to you. I told him he was deluded, of course."

A crash came from upstairs. It sounded like someone had torn the front door off its hinges. She heard the muffled sound of Drake's voice, and a spark of hope flared within her. Jace didn't seem concerned, though. He didn't even turn his head.

"Anyway, I knew he'd be coming back. I knew he'd probably even find you. I couldn't allow him to take you away from me, love." Somewhere, Drake was shouting something about gas. Jace opened his left hand to reveal a lighter.

"So when I got the human blood for you, beloved, it was a present. A going-away present, really. I wanted to have a 'happily ever after,' but I guess this is going to have to do."

She could hear Drake's feet on the stairs. She saw Jace flip the cap off the lighter. *Drake! Get the hell out of here!* she wanted to scream, but even now she was denied that much.

Jace leaned forward to kiss her. "Goodbye, my love," he said, as tears ran from the corners of his eyes. "I wish we could have had longer."

Me too, damn you, she thought. *Me too.*

Even as Drake turned the corner at the bottom of the cellar stairs and lunged, she could hear the rasp of flint striking a fatal spark.

Introduction

"He who bears the brand of Cain shall rule the Earth."
— George Bernard Shaw

Many people have an active interest in the legend of the vampire, to the point of wishing to become a part of it. The idea of the "creature of the night," its myths and legends, is so fascinating that we are captivated by its aura, its power and its romance. The vampire legend is incredibly seductive on several levels.

So what happens to those who become too enamored of that midnight allure, and are seduced by the menacing elements of the World of Darkness? In the Gothic-Punk world, an exceptional few are taken under the vampiric wing to become ghouls. Later, some of these half-humans might become vampires, but for many the cost of humanity, life, the sun and loved ones is one they are not ready to pay. Then again, many human beings don't normally have much of a choice in this sort of decision.

Ghouls are creatures who incorporate the best and the worst of both worlds. They can stay out in the midday sun, taste immortality and even take on the supernatural Disciplines of vampires, but they must often pay with unnatural love. Everything has a price in a ghoul's world, and often she will not see who is paying it.

Vampires build their communities on the backs of their ghouls. Often dismissed and taken for granted, ghouls are the bridge between the worlds of Kindred and kine. Without the help of their Blood Bound retainers, vampires would be prisoners to the rising and setting of the sun, and mostly helpless to affect the sunlit world.

It is no overestimation to state that the Camarilla's strides to preserve the Masquerade would falter or perhaps even fail altogether without ghouls. Nor would it be unfair to say that the Sabbat relies heavily on ghouls; the existence of the Revenant families underscores the usefulness of these half-humans to the *antitribu* (or at least to Clan Tzimisce). Even lowly Anarchs need ghouls for their very survival. Who else could be trusted to haul a vampire on the run out of town under the noon sun, even as the prince's lackeys sweep the streets for her?

Then again, the creation of ghouls exacts a price from Kindred as well. Ghouls may be bound to their Regnants by love, but love can lead to jealousy and hate. Hell hath no fury like a ghoul scorned, and when a ghoul knows all of the secrets of the one who spurned him, the results can be explosive.

This book outlines and describes what is expected of a ghoul in a live-action setting, and details what a player should expect from the World of Darkness. Within these pages are rules, roleplaying hooks and ideas for newcomers to and long-time players of **The Masquerade**. Additionally, Storytellers will find story ideas and clarified rules to use and abuse as they see fit.

Mind's Eye Theatre

Mind's Eye Theatre started years ago, in somebody's backyard, in the park, and during recess on the playground. In essence, it is a game of make-believe, only one set in a very specific place and time. **Mind's Eye Theatre** simply provides rules for resolving arguments on what any given player can or cannot do within the bounds of the game. After all, a tussle over who is right and who is wrong should be the last thing on any roleplayer's agenda; the play's the thing, not the rules. Players who drop out of character to argue over rules interpretations shatter the illusion of the ongoing story, which doesn't help anyone have a good time. The rules of the game are here to streamline the action, not disrupt it.

The foremost priority in **Mind's Eye Theatre** is telling a story. Preferably, the story will not be too convoluted, simple or violent. There is a time and place for all of these things in the World of Darkness, but in measured doses. The best-laid plans often become diverted by the active imaginations of creative roleplayers.

It is therefore the responsibility of the Storyteller to provide a story that can be enjoyed by all her players, not just a few. If a few players want a blood bath, a Storyteller might decide to give it to them, but even mindless violence is bound to get boring after a while. Besides, there are consequences for relentless bloodshed: tedious police investigations, archons asking discomforting questions, Blood Hunts, Inner Circle members demanding a cleansing of the city, and the Sabbat using the chaos to infiltrate what had been a perfectly safe domain.

It is good to remember that rules are there to resolve unclear situations. If the Storyteller makes a decision regarding a rule, such is her right as final arbiter. It is the Storyteller's responsibility to not abuse this power, and the players' responsibility to respect it. Rules in this game are flexible so as to create a game that is ultimately story driven. If a chronicle is being dictated by rules instead of ideas, there are definite problems, and a review of how such a bind was reached is necessary.

The Ghouls

We can feel the pulse of time,
Naked in the wake of lies that suffocate and blind,
We may burn but we will shine.
— My Life With the Thrill Kill Kult, "13 Above the Night"

Ghouls are mortals who have ingested the potent blood of vampires, though not always of their own free will. This powerful elixir carries the curse of Caine's damnation, and infects, to a degree, every creature that consumes it. Most notable among these are human beings, but the effect is not limited to them alone. Animals of all kinds can become ghouls.

In **Mind's Eye Theatre**, the ghoul's part has commonly been passed off to inexperienced players so they can learn the game by watching their Regnants go through the motions (and by staying out of the way of important plots). Unfortunately, this has led to the prevailing notion of the expendable ghoul. This is an unacceptable state of affairs, and is not true to the World of Darkness. Ghouls are neither peripheral to the world of the Kindred, nor are they disposable.

Ghouls fulfill several important roles, all of which are fertile ground for **Mind's Eye Theatre** plots. By playing the roles of servants, ghouls are privy to all sorts of dirty little secrets. They make excellent bodyguards with their command of physical Disciplines; vampires who scoff at the abilities of "lowly" ghouls tempt fate more than they know. Ghouls also serve as envoys to and guardians against the mortal world. This is one of their most important roles, as it is they who tend to their Regnants' daytime business. An efficient ghoul in this position can make her Regnant's unlife much easier; an incompetent one can lead hunters right to the haven door.

Ghouls are always faced with the Blood Bond and the possibility of mistreatment through it. This does not mean, however, that they suffer abuse lightly. Being Blood Bound does not make a ghoul stupid. Ghouls often cope with the Bond better than do vampires, becoming infatuated with their Regnants but not necessarily becoming foolhardy. A ghoul is not going to appreciate being ignored, struck or emotionally abused, and will react as a spurned lover would to such treatment. Jealousy and resentment can even lead a ghoul to question her Bond, eventually causing a true break from her Regnant. Considering the knowledge that many ghouls have, this could prove a fatal problem for their Regnants.

There are also ghouls who, when faced with nothing but abuse, strike back and become vampire hunters, bent on the annihilation of their former masters. Like anyone else, if a ghoul is treated well, she works better and more willingly. Indeed, some ghouls work best alone, while others can learn to share their Regnant's attention with others, if doing so is in the Regnant's best interests. But of course, there are some ghouls whose Regnants might be better off treating them badly, or at least with some caution. Love, especially the false affection of the Blood Bond, can lead to dangerous obsessions.

The most important thing to remember when playing a ghoul is that, with the exception of the Revenant families of the Sabbat, a ghoul is still very much a normal human. The majority of ghouls may still live with loved ones, hold day jobs, pay bills, go to college and so on. Apart from their addiction to vitae, ghouls function like everybody else.

Revenants

Revenants are very different from other ghouls, having been ghouls since their conception. The Revenant families have had vampire blood in their veins for generations, making the half-life the normal state for these strange clans. These creatures are brought up separate from the rest of humanity, and most are unable to exist with vampires or humans.

The difference between a ghoul and a normal mortal lies in the ghoul's longevity and access to vampiric Disciplines. These differences are what set a ghoul apart from the unknowing part of kine society, both physically and socially. And these differences are largely responsible for even the most stable ghoul's eventual alienation from normal life; the ghoul knows she is a changed creature, no longer just one of the herd. This transition may or may not fit in with her or her loved ones' personal beliefs, ethics or moral values, and the pain this conflict can bring proves unbearable for some.

Instructions for the Proper Use of This Book

This book should broaden the perspectives of both Storytellers and players. It fleshes out a vital part of the World of Darkness that, until now, has been largely taken for granted. Ghouls are truly the backbone of Kindred society, enabling vampires to extend their influence to the sunlit hours. This makes ghouls quite necessary for vampires who have political interests — courts of law, businesses and elections are all daytime operations — and for those who have nothing but mischief on their minds. If a vampire wants to affect something — anything — in the mortal world while the sun is high, he probably has to use a ghoul to do it. Considering the sheer variety of ways in which a vampire is likely to want to interact with the world during daytime hours, that leaves an awful lot for ghouls to do.

Ghouls are perfect characters for new players who know little about **Mind's Eye Theatre** but who would like to play immediately. The opportunity to learn while playing is invaluable, and the very nature of "new ghoul" roles explains any "out-of-character" awkwardness or ignorance.

On the other hand, experienced **Mind's Eye Theatre** players will find ghouls to have a capacity for multilevel play, as they can interact with more denizens of the World of Darkness than just vampires. After all, who's to say that a changeling, werewolf or wraith can't cut a deal, and what of the ambitious Tremere ghoul who's selling his Regnant's vitae to a local mage?

Nor should players be the only ones having fun with ghouls. Storytellers can use ghouls as antagonists or to perpetuate storylines or puncture vampiric arrogance and to continue game action during daylight hours.

This book will show that ghouls are much more than slaves or convenient juice bags. It gives easy-to-follow rules and suggestions on how to create and play ghouls. Remember, though, the most important thing is the story! The only real instructions to be paid special heed to are the ones that you come up with. So Storytellers, feel free to disregard that which you disagree with and go wild with what you like. The only limitations to a story are the ones *you* set.

The Only Rules That Matter

These are the most important rules of **MET**, the only ones that absolutely must be obeyed. Obviously, there are a lot of people out there who either don't know or don't care that it's just a game. On the other hand, there are some people who take the game far too seriously. By following these rules, you provide yourself with ammunition against the former and protect yourself and your game against the latter. Both groups are equally dangerous to a solid **Mind's Eye Theatre** troupe, and these rules are designed to make certain that offenders are given as little opportunity as possible to interfere.

#1 – It's only a game.

This is by far the most important rule. It is only a game. If a character slides into the Beast, if a plot falls apart, if a rival wins the day — it's still only a game. Don't take things too seriously, as that will spoil not only your enjoyment but also the enjoyment of everyone else. If the line between you and your character blurs, step back a bit and take some time off. If you see another player confusing himself with his character, get in contact with the Storyteller. Someone who takes your play too seriously isn't healthy for a game, or for his fellow players.

Remember to leave the game behind when it ends. **The Masquerade** is a lot of fun; spending time talking about the game is great. However, remember that not everyone you know is going to want to hear about your character; many will have no idea what you're talking about. Plus, other players may want time off. Getting together with the rest of the "household" to bitch about the Regnant over pizza is one thing. It's entirely another to wake someone at 6:00 A.M. on Sunday to ask about putting her Influences toward your pet project.

#2 – No touching.

No touching means no touching. None. Ever. There's simply too much of a chance that someone will get excited in the heat of combat or some other stressful situation and proceed to hurt themselves or someone else, however accidentally.

This rule also applies to running, jumping, swinging on chandeliers through sheets of plate glass, and other overly energetic behaviors that can result in injuries. This game is called **Mind's Eye Theatre** for a reason. If you can imagine yourself as a bloodsucking sycophant, then imagining yourself running when you're actually walking should be a snap.

#3 – No weapons as props.

Props are a wonderful way to make a game more real. However, real weapons or anything that even looks like a real weapon (and we're talking sword canes, peace-bonded claymores, trained attack gerbils, matte-black painted waterguns, and sword-shaped toothpicks from martinis) are a definite no-no. There are too many paranoid people in the world who will see a prop gun and mistake it for a real one, or who will see a costume dagger and start screaming for the police. Plus, there's the ever-present threat of someone getting hurt. No matter how much having a sword suits your character concept, leave the real thing at home. If you bring it, it's inevitable that the one time you unsheathe it to show it off, some idiot will come pelting around the corner and neatly skewer himself. The illusion is not worth risking anyone's safety.

#4 – No drugs or drinking.

This is a real no-brainer. Drugs and alcohol help distance you from yourself. Roleplaying gives you the chance to be someone else. Why go to all the trouble of creating another persona to inhabit if you're just going to wander out of that persona in a haze?

On a more serious note, players who are impaired through drugs or alcohol represent a danger to other players and a threat to the flow and mood of the game. There's nothing wrong with *playing* a character who's drunk or stoned, but actually bringing drugs or alcohol into a game is going too far, not to mention the fact that it's possibly illegal. Don't do it.

#5 – Feel free to ignore or adjust any of the rules in this book if it will make your game better.

We at White Wolf call this "The Golden Rule." Obviously, it should be applied within limits, and rules changes should be consistent throughout a story or chronicle. If your troupe finds a way to handle Celerity that works better for it than what's set in **The Masquerade**, by all means go for it.

#6 – Remember, not everyone is playing.

While "freaking the mundanes" can be fun, a game can be unnerving or even frightening to passersby. Be considerate of nonplayers in your vicinity. If you're in a public area, make sure that your gameplay doesn't alarm random civilians to the point where security or the police are called. Explaining to some "concerned citizens" at 3 A.M. that your goblet of "blood" is just a glass of *very* red fruit punch is an exercise in futility.

#7 – Have fun.

Not "win." Not "Go out and kill everyone else." Just "Have fun," because it's not about how the game ends, it's about everything that happens along the way.

Chapter Two:
Ghoul Types

One cannot raise the bottom of society without benefiting everyone above.
— Michael Harrington, *The Other America*

The types of ghouls are as varied as the monsters that a child imagines to be under her bed. Forming a far-from-homogenous society, ghouls serve, fight and live for their own reasons. However, the ghoul population can be divided into rough thirds: Servitors, revenants and Hunters. Each sort of ghoul has its own motivations, and humanity at large would deny relations to most ghouls. They are outside of humanity, tainted by the touch of Caine. The Beast prowls the perimeter of every ghoul's soul, looking for a way in, and is all too ready to pounce when it finds one.

Of course, each ghoul thinks he has a handle on his situation, and can't possibly comprehend what the other types of ghouls are up to. The average Servitor would rather die than be on his own, while the average Hunter would accept destruction before the Bond. As for revenants, the lifestyles of "normal" ghouls is so far from their own that it is unimaginable.

And so nights are whiled away by these human drinkers of vitae, each one passing the decades in her own way. Servitors slave away willingly for their immortal masters. Hunters subdue or slay for their fixes. On the fringes of ghoul society, revenants lose any semblance to humanity that their ancestors might have once had. And in the shadows skulk other groups, the Arcianists and the Talons of Black Rage. There is a multitude of paths from which to choose, even for the Bound.

A Note

For more detailed information on ghouls, see **Ghouls: Fatal Addiction** for **Vampire: The Masquerade**. This chapter gives the basics for purposes of live roleplaying. The following material is written with ease of play in mind. Any background information in **Fatal Addiction** supersedes the material in this chapter at the Storyteller's discretion.

The Servitors

Mainly thought of as classic "Renfield" ghouls, Servitors have been grossly misrepresented over the years. In some ways, this is to their advantage; vampires automatically expect absolute devotion from them. The majority of Servitor ghouls possess Architect, Sycophant and Visionary Natures, but others are possible.

Most Servitors spend their lives serving their Regnants through a broad array of duties. They are protectors, confidants, stewards and, perhaps most importantly, ambassadors to the mortal world. The vast majority like where they are and what they do. They have nothing but contempt for the ruck and run of mortals, viewing themselves as a step above those who don't have Kindred vitae on their lips. Vampire strategies for dealing with the mortal world are often modified or even composed by willing Servitors, who are more in touch with the living than are their masters. Politicians, judges, advertising executives, lawyers and real-estate agents make excellent Servitors. A great many Servitors are convinced that they are on the fast track to true immortality, but even those who are content to remain ghouls actively enjoy the perks that their supernatural existences offer. For most Servitors, power comes at fair price, and they'd gladly pay it again.

On the other hand, some Servitors actively work toward the day when they can turn their formidable knowledge against their masters. This ingratitude is usually born not of hatred, but of sheer boredom. As the decades grind on, quasi-immortality does not always wear well on a living creature. Ennui wages a harsh war against these ghouls, and they are at times ill-prepared for battle. For some Servitors, this rebellious streak survives even under the compact of the Blood Bond, becoming a subconscious rejection of slavery. Disgruntled Servitors do not always mean their Regnants harm, but many do. Others set events in motion against their Regnants just so they can swoop in and "save" their beloved masters, hopefully garnering affection and attention from the suitably grateful vampires.

Competition in the household is the other great problem that faces Servitor ghouls. Rarely is a single ghoul sufficient to meet all of a vampire's needs, and in many cases there are at least three Bound to a given Regnant. Rivalries often flare as ghouls fight for their Regnant's attention; supernaturally induced jealousy is as virulent (if not more so) as the natural kind. When selecting their ghouls, most vampires rarely consider whether or not their servants are going to get along. They simply look for mortals who can get the job done. This policy often backfires, though; ghouls can spend more time squabbling than accomplishing their tasks. Such competition can even turn deadly; ghouls can mount their own Jyhads or be destroyed by Regnants who grow tired of all the bickering.

In their favor, Servitors can draw on their Regnants' ample resources. Furthermore, when they can agree with one another, ghouls belonging to a single vampire don't usually mind sharing their personal Influences, so long as the privilege isn't abused. Valued Servitors, like any important resource, are frequently protected by their owners, and this provides them with some degree of safety in the shadow society that they move in. In addition, many Servitors need never worry about necessities like food, lodging and the like, as Regnants often provide these things through simple necessity of maintaining a ghoul staff.

In the end, though, Servitors are handpicked by vampires to serve. It stands to reason, then, that vampires pick mortals who have something to offer. Servitors without useful skills or contacts are a waste of vitae, and are not tolerated.

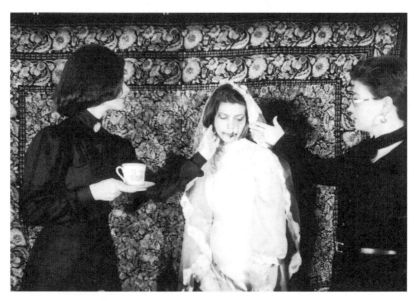

Unfortunately, not all vampires make good masters, and mistreatment of Servitors has become legendary among ghouls. They hear tales of abuse and torment, and eventually even the most pampered ghouls may glance uneasily at their Regnants. After being dangled as bait for an enemy or forced to run missions through hazardous territory enough times, even the most loyal Servitor begins to question the wisdom of continuing her current employment. Particularly vicious abuse can spark a ghoul to open revolt; a servant who is held loyal only by the frayed tethers of the Blood Bond may not be held for long. Less openly rebellious Servitors can act like the djinni of Arabian myth and conduct their Regnants' business by the letter of the command, not the spirit. This game can be dangerous for both parties. A vampire whose commands aren't followed to specification may find herself in hot water, while a ghoul who is willfully disobedient too many times can find his servitude at a violent end.

Yet the vast majority of Servitors are happy in bondage. Decades of being denied true immortality or years of abuse can slowly sour a Servitor on her station, but almost no Servitor would change her status to be a mere human.

Stereotypes

Hunters — These idiots have no idea what they're doing. If they'd settle down and take to one master, they might be happier. Never let the hard cases into the house, but if you can see the softness in a Hunter's eyes, you just might be able to turn him back to his proper place. Careful with the hard sell, though; most Hunters can spot it, and resent it. "Traitor" is probably the nicest name you'll hear after that.

Revenants — Never hesitate to inform your Regnant if you ever meet one of these disgusting monsters. Death isn't permanent enough for these beasts!

Kindred — Our masters know what is best for us. After all, they've had a long time to learn about life, haven't they? It's best to keep them happy and do as they say. Just look at all they give us in return — maybe even the ultimate gift.

Sabbat — Never, ever believe anything a Sabbat vampire says to you. No matter what one offers, he's lying. If you're approached by a Sabbat vampire, tell your Regnant immediately. Don't try to be a hero. Play along to gather all the information you can, instead.

Mortals — They have no idea what they're missing, and it's best to keep it that way. Can you imagine the chaos if the *hoi polloi* got access to the things we do? No, it's far better to observe them from above than to try to elevate them. Poor bastards.

Hunters

Hunters are divided into two classes: those who hunt to kill and those who hunt to survive. A killer often has a past blackened by a vampire who killed a loved one, attacked the Hunter, or abused him as a Servitor. Rarer are the religious or moralistic fanatics who wander their way into ghouldom. These killers are intent on stamping out "evil," and attempt to use the Devil's own tools against him. As witch-hunter ghouls come from every walk of life, their array of possible Natures is astounding.

Some Hunter ghouls slay every vampire they meet without mercy, delaying the *coup de grace* just long enough to take their victims' blood. The *raison d'être* for this behavior is, supposedly, that only vampire blood enables these noble Hunters to continue their war with the bloodsuckers. Ask any vampire-killer and he will swear up and down that he regards his addiction to blood as a necessary evil, and that if he could be free of it, he would. Of course, most of these Hunters have stashed away huge stocks of Blood Traits to support both their hunts and their habits. There are even rumors of elder ghouls, their lifespans prolonged by centuries, who pick off young Hunters to reduce competition for the precious vitae.

Hunters and Vampires

Many vampires who wish to dispose of rivals without tempting the consequences of diablerie turn to Hunter ghouls to do their dirty work. Few of these vampires actively work with their unsuspecting hatchetmen. Instead, such vampiric quislings drop hints or have their Servitors leave clues for the hapless Hunters to follow to rivals' havens. Most Hunters follow a trail, congratulate themselves on their cleverness, and never suspect that they've been played like violins. Only a few very experienced Hunters can recognize such schemes.

The greatest advantage that Hunter-killer ghouls have is their organizational capacity. Most, if not all, have a vast network of contacts; a lively trade in information, tactics and tools occurs whenever Hunters cross paths. There are even societies of Hunter-killer ghouls, though most groups of this sort tend to have lifespans of under a decade. Casualty ratios and inevitable infiltrations by Servitor ghouls render even the most effective collections of killers impotent after a few years.

There are also Hunter ghouls who do not kill their prey. The equivalent of "Sandman" vampires, these Hunters stalk vampires for vitae to support their own immortality, and nothing more. They have no ties to one another, though some have formed working relationships with vampires. Indomitable survivors and loners by choice, these Hunters actively shy away from the Bond. They drink from the same font twice only if in the direst of straits, and many claim that death is preferable to the Bond.

Harvester Hunters (as these are called) have a number of stalking techniques that closely mirror those of vampires themselves. Some prefer to slip into a marked vampire's haven and secretly draw blood from the unsuspecting victim. Others prefer seduction. There are even those who prefer to assault vampires physically and take their vitae, but most of this sort don't live very long.

Hunting the hunters can be an extremely complicated proposition for ghouls who are out for blood instead of ash. Most witch-hunters have the simple aim of annihilating their targets; Harvesters have to get in close and stay there in order to get what they need. It goes without saying that there are far safer places to be than at a vampire's bedside, IV in hand. While these ghouls do have the traditional Kindred advantage that their prey is usually unaware that it is being hunted (How many vampires really worry about mortals hunting them for their blood?), the actual hunt is fraught with difficulties and dangers. Hunters using a Casanova approach have a hard time picking up marks when vampires have so many other willing victims to choose from. Sandman Hunters are also faced with paranoid vampires' exasperating and potentially fatal daylight security. Indeed, considering the risk-to-reward ratio for this sort of hunting, it is surprising how many ghouls make a go of it.

The only tried-and-true method these ghouls have (and it is a surprisingly effective one) involves befriending Servitors with the hope of being permitted to drop by a haven for a quick sip. The Servitor who agrees to this arrangement had better be quite sure that he's indispensable. A vampire who awakens weaker than she ought to be will have some pointed questions for her favorite ghouls, and may not like the answers she receives. In addition, many Hunters tell stories about throwing themselves through second-story windows in panicked attempts to get away from light-sleeping vampires.

Over the years the two Hunter factions of ghouls have grown increasingly aware of each another. Neither is comfortable with the other's approaches or tactics, but the war against the common enemy takes precedence over any internecine strife.

Hunter Stereotypes

Servitors — Slaves, the lot of them. They're weak. Some of them can't help it because of the Bond, but most love licking vampire boots. If you can hide your disgust, a houseboy can be helpful in getting a pint in a tough situation, but that's as far as it goes.

Revenants — They're the reason I don't believe in God.

Kindred — We can't live with 'em, we can't live without 'em, and I for one don't much like either option.

Sabbat — No mercy; they won't show you any. We're not even a resource to them, we're a meal!

Mortals — In the grand scheme of things, they just don't matter, except as food for vampires. Otherwise, they're nothing more than speed bumps on the road we're all taking to Hell.

The Revenant Families

Created over a millennium ago through pacts made with the Tzimisce, these four ghoul families are born with vampire blood in their veins. Reveling in debauchery and sadism above and beyond what their service to the Fiends demands, Revenants have a foul reputation even among the Sabbat.

Revenants don't need vampire blood to survive their first 300 years. The Tzimisce blood that the families are infused with has changed their genetic structure. Revenants seeking more than three centuries' existence do require

dosages of vampire blood, but not many last even 300 years. The foul pleasures that these creatures revel in do have their dangers.

The revenant families are not in the safest of positions, despite their advantage of not needing the blood to reach a great age. Loyal to the Sabbat, incapable of true interaction with mortals, and without hope of ever being allowed into the Camarilla, revenants' actions are tightly circumscribed. They are trapped in an organization that allows for no growth, and in which the majority of their putative allies would like nothing better than to obliterate them. Four of the original eight revenant families have already been "culled," and there are constant rumors that an additional purge of one family or another is coming. Despite the talents, resources and apparent unimpeachable loyalty of the revenant families, the vast majority of Sabbat vampires would still destroy every last one of them; only the backing of Clan Tzimisce sustains the ghoul clans. However, the Tzimisce support the four families more in principle than anything else these days (by right of Sabbat law, a single mistake can earn a ghoul immediate and gory release from this mortal coil).

The four families of revenant ghouls include the Bratoviches ("Monsters"), the Grimaldis ("Puppets"), the Obertuses ("Hermits") and the Zantosas ("Trash"). Each family gets along with the others tempestuously at best, but there are occasional intermarriages that serve as elaborate displays of so-called unity and goodwill. The products of such marriages uniformly suffer derision and abuse from the families involved.

The Bratoviches

The Bratovich family is widely considered the most disturbing of all of the revenant clans, and the Monsters are now all but completely ignored by the Sabbat. The only service these ghouls still provide to the sect at large is the raising and training of hideous ghouled hounds for hunting. Most Bratovich households keep large private kennels for personal use, and for disposing of "accidents."

Pragmatic in their dealings with vampires, the Bratoviches have always been interested in staying on the winning side of any conflict. The one exception to the infamous Bratovich shifting loyalty is the hatred the entire family has for Lupines; Bratovich excellence at hunting and slaughtering werewolves is astonishing. Their keen understanding of Lupine tactics has been the downfall of many a pack that has wandered too close to one of the family's large, dilapidated estates. Of course, the atrocities that the Bratoviches practice — cannibalism, vivisection and the like — produce enough of a Wyrm-taint to lure in altruistic or unwary Lupines. Few werewolves realize what they're getting into, and fewer get out alive.

While not actively anachronistic, these ghouls are reclusive and possess few modern conveniences like televisions, radios or microwave ovens. On the other hand, Bratoviches are compulsive pack rats. The Monsters' estates are absolutely filled to overflowing with the junk that the households have collected over the decades. Neither personal hygiene nor landscaping is high on the list of Bratovich priorities. Family estates and their tenants tend to be equally repulsive in appearance (not to mention odor).

Oddly enough, Bratovich children attend public schools like normal children, but also attend classes at home. Toxicology, animal handling, torture and other extremely liberal arts are at the top of each semester's schedule.

Vampire blood is such an integral part of the Monsters that they actually have a clan weakness. Monsters are prone to frenzy. In terms of game mechanics, this flaw functions exactly like the weakness of the Brujah clan. For more information, see **Laws of the Night**.

Bratovich Stereotypes

Servitors — Stupid pawns. Let 'em lead you to their masters, then feed 'em to your dogs.

Hunters — They're kinda fun to bother, but not much of a threat. A Hunter will usually attack until you fuse his mouth and nose shut, then he'll just kinda fall over and wriggle a bit before he suffocates. Take pictures to show the kids!

Kindred — Show off that good-neighbor side until they're not looking, then plan a barbecue!

Sabbat — Be on your best behavior around Sabbat types, because they can kick our butts if they decide we're getting uppity. It means eating dirt sometimes, but it also means living to see the sunrise.

Mortals — Breeding stock, if that. Most get one whiff and decide to back off. Smart people.

The Grimaldis

Of all the revenant clans, the Grimaldis who work the best in the mortal world. Blending in with an ease born of years of practice, the Puppets are perhaps the most human of the revenant families. Many even develop additional Humanity Traits, as opposed to members of the other revenant families (who frequently lose those Traits with appalling speed). Most of this relatively enlightened existence comes from the intense contact the Grimaldis have with mortals throughout their lives. Grimaldi children go through normal public or private schools and colleges while being groomed for lifetimes of servitude. Most adult Grimaldi actually function as part of the regular work force, as their utility to the Tzimisce extends far beyond their homes and pets.

This family serves as a link between the Sabbat and the mortal world; more than one vampire has referred to the Grimaldi as the Servitors of the Sabbat. In essence, the Grimaldi are in charge of maintaining a masquerade for the Sabbat. With the support of their vampiric allies and human contacts, they control most of the media in Sabbat-held cities. The family is also quite proficient at the fine arts of blackmail and bribery, a fact which routinely puts mortal movers and shakers firmly in the Grimaldi pocket.

These ghouls are both highly organized and incredibly wealthy, to the point where they almost rival the Ventrue and Giovanni in influence. Indeed, Puppet cunning and skill at high finance is a match for those of the Ventrue; more than one Blue Blood has been appalled to discover that the up-and-comer that he had targeted for the Embrace was in fact a Grimaldi. (**Note**: When creating a Grimaldi, it is always a good idea to purchase as many Influences as possible.)

The only thing preventing a Grimaldi from gaining the normal maximum of Humanity Traits is something inherent to the family: Every last Puppet is Blood Bound to a Sabbat bishop or archbishop. This tight rein is viewed as a necessary precaution. After all, Grimaldi ghouls have both the resources and the capability to do severe damage should they develop sufficient incentive. However, at this point the mandatory Bond is almost never more than symbolic, as the Grimaldis would seem to be perfectly loyal. A Sabbat "patron," as a Grimaldi refers to her blood donor, seldom calls on (or even calls for) this Blood Bond. It is the Grimaldi themselves who submit willingly to the Bond. They make this gesture out of both respect and loyalty, perhaps to convince the Sabbat that they are worth keeping around.

Grimaldi Stereotypes

Servitors — A mixed bag is the best way of describing these folks. The good ones are probably the smartest ghouls. They know how to get what they want, not to mention what's really worth wanting. The worst ones might as well be dirt.

Hunters — It's just stupid to kill that which makes you what you are. Besides, ghouls who make too much noise are reminiscent of the proverbial nail that stands out, begging to be hammered down. These ghouls make a lot of noise.

Kindred — It's ironic that we're often compared to Camarilla ghouls — or vampires. We're all about business while they're all about self-aggrandizement. If a Cam vampire targets you for the Embrace, remove his illusions. Otherwise, things will get sticky.

Sabbat — Stay on their good side and they'll ignore you. That's all you really want from them, so you can get on with your life without being tangled up in their nasty power struggles. Tzimisce versus Lasombra versus *antitribu* versus — who cares? Take care of your own business.

Mortals — Sometimes you have to envy their ignorance. Other times you have to pity them. They're caught up in a game they don't even understand.

The Obertuses

The Obertus family has earned the nickname "Hermits" for its members' extensive research into esoteric knowledge and lore. These ghouls reside in small communities composed entirely of family members, usually far from the hustle and bustle of big cities. Most Obertus settlements are located in New England, the American Midwest and Central America, but other villages are scattered all over the globe. While there's nothing overtly odd about an Obertus village, visitors are not welcome, and enough odd things will happen during the course of a single day (or night) to drive off even the most insensitive tourist.

The Obertuses are the quiet ones of the revenant families, and their obsessive search for information has taken them in some strange directions. Although their relentlessly rational approach (not to mention strict hewing to the Paths of Enlightenment) has kept the majority of family members sane in the face of even the foulest of discoveries, a few relatives passed beyond the gates of sanity long ago. The problem is that you can never tell who the mad ones are….

It is said, and rightly so, that some of the world's greatest scholars are Obertus revenants. While Obertus children have no formal education, they do receive private tutoring from family members, who are more than qualified to teach. This phase of Hermit education lasts until a child becomes old enough to seek his own teachers and fields of study. At this point, his life-long quest for true knowledge begins. Only death ends that search and the Obertuses hoard every bit of knowledge they acquire. The eldest members of the family have accumulated astonishing libraries over the centuries, and young Obertus ghouls may — if they are properly respectful — occasionally be permitted to access these tremendous resources.

The Obertus family retains close ties to Clan Tzimisce, but seldom actively involves itself in vampiric affairs. However, the Obertuses do serve the information brokers of the Sabbat, and have successfully infiltrated the Society of Leopold, the Arcanum and a number of other esoteric organizations. Of special interest to these ghoulish moles is information on Caine, demons, Lupines and mages.

The weakness of the family is a predictable one: intellectual obsession. Once an Obertus is hooked on a subject, she'll follow an information trail to the ends of the earth, regardless of danger or cost.

Obertus Stereotypes

Servitors — At least these ghouls make themselves useful. I really have no interest in them beyond that.

Hunters — They are both pragmatic and illogical. If the blood is what they desire, there are more efficient ways of obtaining it. If they wish to kill vampires, there are more effective ways of doing that, too. However, the degrees of success they have achieved in both regards means that their methods warrant closer observation.

Kindred — Many are vast fonts of knowledge. Those who are not are best treated well until they move on. The fewer questions they ask about what we are doing, the better. We have no wish to be caught between the two sects when they clash over the secrets they think we possess.

Sabbat — Which Sabbat are we talking about? The old members of the sect are gracious, knowledgeable and intelligent. They respect what we do, and we have no difficulties serving them. The young Sabbat are rude, crude, loud things with no respect for knowledge or those who preserve it. Our doors are shut to these fools.

Mortals — They are useful for experimentation, among other things. Few live long enough to accumulate any knowledge worth seeking, but sometimes it is the flame that burns out most quickly that shines the brightest.

The Zantosas

Unquestionably the prime hedonists of the revenant families, the Zantosas love pleasure and excess above all else. A Zantosa will inevitably be preceded by his family's reputation into any social situation. Every revenant has stories about the lengths to a Zantosa will go to in order to satisfy some perversion or other. Such tales are almost the equivalent of "light-bulb jokes." On the other hand, the Trash may be hedonists, but they are not idle ones. The family is fabulously wealthy, and has a genetically transmitted streak of irrepressible cruelty that makes it less of a joke and more of a dangerous curiosity to those who meet its members.

Descended from a cluster of noble houses in Eastern Europe, the Zantosas served as a sort-of breeding pool for the Tzimisce. For centuries these ghouls worked as spies in Europe's most powerful courts, and those who served the Tzimisce well were rewarded on rare occasions with the Embrace. Well trusted and unquestionably loyal, the gaggle of families (now so thoroughly intermarried as to be essentially one lineage) followed the Tzimisce into the fledgling Sabbat. Many members of the family were Embraced to serve as cannon fodder during the Sabbat-Camarilla wars.

Thanks to their grasp of Vicissitude, the Trash are easily the most attractive of the ghoul families. Dancing on the cutting edge of technology and hedonism, most Zantosas dabble in drugs (dealing or using) as well as other assorted antisocial or illegal behaviors. It is very important to a Zantosa to have the latest technological toys and marvels, and just as important to have traveled to all of the "hot" spots. A Zantosa who's a season behind the times in anything is as good as forgotten by the rest of the family, at least until she catches up with the social whirl.

Zantosas tend to keep spotless homes and stables. Their stables, however, also serve as pantries; these ghouls have a peculiar taste for horseflesh. A

dinner invitation to a Zantosa residence is not for the faint of heart or weak of stomach.

Culinary perversion is not the most closely held secret of the Zantosas. That honor falls to the fact that they, alone among of all the revenant families, guard the slumbering Tzimisce Antediluvian. Were this to become known, the family would be exterminated and the Antediluvian exhumed, undoubtedly to disastrous effect.

The Zantosas' greatest weakness is their addictions. If given intense pleasure by anything, a Zantosa must make a Static Challenge or immediately acquire an addiction to the source.

Zantosa Stereotypes

Servitors — Booooooooring. You can't liven up a Servitor's day with anything… except maybe slipping acid into her groceries.

Hunters — They're not exactly party animals, and they always have such serious faces! Always thinking about their next infusion of blood-this and next-hunt-that; they make lousy conversation. Even we're not that bad.

Kindred — The fangdaddies are fun, if not exactly safe to be around. Still, life's never dull when you're palling around with the living dead! Besides, the look on a Cammy vamp's face when he realizes he's been necking with a revenant is priceless!

Sabbat — Some of these vampires have a sense of humor that matches ours, and we'll work with them when it doesn't throw our own schedules out of whack. Avoid the "destroy-the-Camarilla" types. They'll waste us as quickly as their enemies.

Mortals — Wheeee! Humans are fun, fun, fun to play with, but they break easily. Too bad.

Other Ghouls

The Arcianist Historical Society

The Arcianist Historical Society has come far and changed much in the last few years. The core of the group consists of five renegade Tremere ghouls who, fueled by the vitae of an imprisoned seventh-generation vampire, plot to destroy the vampires of the world. Protected by a series of spells that disguise their true natures, these five ghouls serve as a clearinghouse of ghoul candidates for the Ventrue of the Camarilla. The society has links with the Sabbat as well, but its main business is with the Camarilla.

While the ghouls that the Arcianists supply are uniformly excellent — intelligent, talented and attractive — they do come with one hidden feature. Each Arcianist-trained ghoul is implanted with a post-hypnotic suggestion. This hidden programming ensures that on a certain date, each ghoul that the

Society provides will dial a phone number and detail the defenses of her Regnant's haven. What follows will almost certainly be academic, not to mention bloody.

The ghouls of the society never deal directly with their vampire customers. Instead, they use their secretary Jeanette as a front. Most of the Arcianists' customers respect this desire for privacy. The rest contribute to the light of the sunrise.

The Society does deal with the Sabbat, and the groups occasionally cooperate on hunting down a particularly meddlesome Camarilla vampire. In the end, however, the five ghouls of the Society don't intend to spare even their erstwhile allies from their coming purge.

Two members of the society possess True Faith, and another is rumored to have an artifact called the Undying Heart. All sorts of rumors surround the latter, but one piece of information is cold, hard fact: If the Tzimisce knew of the Heart's location, they'd stop at nothing to retrieve it.

Society ghouls have acquired a method for breaking Blood Bonds, beyond other achievements. This knowledge, along with the existence of the imprisoned Tremere *antitribu* in the basement, is kept under the closest of wraps. Either tidbit would be explosive enough to bring down considerable vampiric wrath on the society. No matter how potent their defenses, the Arcianists are not capable of holding off a determined assault.

While it is not recommended that players take the parts of the five leaders of the Arcianist Historical Society, ghouls recruited by the Arcianists make excellent characters. For more information on the Arcianists, see **Antagonists**.

The Talons of Black Rage

The Talons are the result of an eugenics project performed by a small number of Lasombra, without the consent of *Les Amies Noir*. (The last such project resulted in the creation of the Kiasyd bloodline. Understandably, the clan elders are not eager to repeat that sort of blunder). The Talons were bred for the express purpose of infiltrating the Black Hand and destroying it from within. Their secondary mission was (and is) to counter the efforts of the revenant families within the Sabbat, forcing the Tzimisce to disband or destroy those ghouls. Most Sabbat — even most Lasombra — are unaware of the Talons' existence. The Lasombra progenitors of these ghouls intend to keep it that way.

To date there are 13 members of the Talons: seven men and six women. All are followers of the Path of Power and the Inner Voice, and all are familiar with Obtenebration, Chimerstry and assorted martial arts. Five generations of Talons have been bred, and each successive brood is increasingly deadly. The existing Talons are each more than a match for most neonate vampires.

For more information on the Talons, see **Antagonists**.

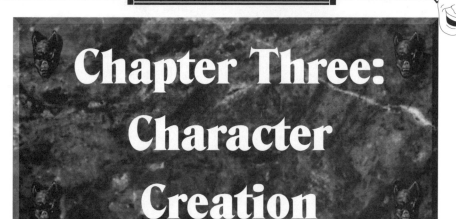

Chapter Three: Character Creation

People seem not to see that their opinion of the world is also a confession of character.
— R. W. Emerson, *The Conduct of Life*

Warning

This section is a quick-and-dirty guide to ghoul creation. We assume that you are familiar with the **Mind's Eye Theatre** character creation process from **The Masquerade: Second Edition** or **Laws of the Night**. If you are not familiar with either of those books, read one of them before attempting to use the following material.

Any lists of Traits, Merits or Flaws that are not included in this book can be found in **Laws of the Night** or **The Masquerade: Second Edition**.

Character Concept: Who Are You?

It has often been said that a story with incredible characters and a horrible plot will go farther than one with an outstanding plot and one-dimensional characters. The key to an interesting story is characterization, and good characterization begins with building a character from the ground up. After all, in creating a character you are in a sense creating a person, and you need to consider exactly who this person is. This process does not consist of slapping a name on a list of adjectives. You have to think about what makes this person so interesting to you that you want to *be* her for an evening (or several evenings). If there's nothing interesting about your character, you're not going to be interested in being — or playing — her.

Identifying with your character is important, so you might want to draw on subjects that you're interested in to add depth to her background. If you're interested in a particular historical period, consider giving your character some involvement in the important events of that era. If you like rock climbing, even if you've never so much as scaled a particularly tall anthill, consider adding it to your character's list of interests.

Once you have a basic idea of who your character is, start imagining her history. Figure out who she was and what happened in her past that made her who she is today. Details like where she was born, her economic circumstances, and the time period and setting of her upbringing have great impact on your character's life.

Your character may have entered the world of vampires at any point in history that makes sense (the height of the Sumerian empire, for example, is right out). If your character was born in America in the '50s and became a ghoul in the '70s, she must have been profoundly affected by all the political upheavals she lived through. The Vietnam War, Watergate, the disillusionment of a country, conspiracies — all of these should be reflected in her outlook (which may have crystallized somewhat at the moment she was made a ghoul).

What's in a Name?

An important part of any character is her name. While you may think naming is the least important part of character design, the name you choose for your ghoul is the one you're going to be answering to — perhaps for a long time. A good name also goes a long way toward cementing a character's image. If you doubt that, consider this: Would you be in any way, shape or form terrified of a Brujah named Alouicious?

If you have trouble naming your character, books of baby names are useful. Many provide lists of names from other countries and cultures, assuming you decide to give your character a background from further afield than the local suburbs. Nicknames are fun, too, but ones like Slash or Blade get redundant fast — odds are the local vampiric community already supports at least three guys with similar monosyllabic handles.

Consider your character's biological age, particularly the year in which she stopped aging. Ghouls can be of any age, although small children and nonagenarians are not recommended. Your character's apparent age dictates how people treat her, and can affect her outlook on life. If your character became a ghoul at age 14, all the fake IDs in the world aren't going to help her get into a bar. If your character is middle-aged, she might get more respect on one level, but people are going to underestimate her physical capabilities.

Once you have decided on a time and place as the starting point for your character, think about what events have shaped your character's life. Writing up a brief synopsis is helpful. It doesn't have to be a 12-volume epic, but it's good to get some grounding that will give you material to work with later. Consider the questions: Did your character come from a dysfunctional family? Was her upbringing perfectly mundane? Was she wealthy? What did her parents do? Was she raised by a single parent? How far did she get in school? What special talents does she possess? Is she a citizen or an immigrant? Did she have siblings? Does she have a job? Is she married? What are her interests?

Hopefully these questions will fuel your creative processes and bring you to the moment of truth: the entrance of a Regnant into your character's life. Odds are your character will enter the game as a ghoul, so you need to decide a few things about your Regnant and your character's relationship with him.

Steps of Ghoul Character Creation

Step One: Inspiration — Who are you?
— Choose your Regnant
— Choose a Nature and Demeanor

Step Two: Attributes — What are your basic capabilities?
— Prioritize Attributes (seven Primary, five Secondary and three Tertiary)

Step Three: Advantages — What do you know?
— Choose five Abilities
— Choose one Discipline (Celerity, Fortitude or Potence only)
— Choose three Influences
— Choose Humanity Traits

Step Four: Last Touches — Fill in the details.
— Assign Blood Traits
— Assign Willpower Traits
— Record Status Trait of *Recognized*
— Choose Negative Traits (if any)

Step Five: Spark of Life — Narrative descriptions

Choosing Your Regnant

Before you begin choosing Attributes, Abilities and Disciplines, you have to decide who your Regnant is. Choosing another player's vampire character or a nonplayer character is best for many reasons. With another player as a Regnant, you automatically have someone to roleplay with, and a means to introduce your character to the plots already in progress. Furthermore, when that time of the month rolls around, your character has someone to give her blood.

You also need to decide how your character feels about her Regnant. Does her Regnant mistreat her? Is she in love with him? Is she jealous of his other ghouls? Defining the Regnant-Thrall relationship early on is vital.

You also need to figure out what you do for your Regnant, and why he keeps you around. If the vampire has other ghouls, you should establish your relationships with them. The history of your dealings with your Regnant need to be laid down, including his reasons for taking you under his vampiric wing. Everything that you come up with should be cleared with a Storyteller, but once this groundwork is established, you're ready for the hard part: assigning Traits.

Nature and Demeanor

Your Nature is your character's true self, which is often hidden from the world. Your ghoul's Demeanor, however, is the façade she wears when dealing with others. A character's Nature and Demeanor can be the same or widely different, depending on her approach to the world. A complete listing of Natures and Demeanors can be found in **The Masquerade: Second Edition** (p. 19), but you don't have to limit yourself to the ones in print. With Storyteller approval, you can come up with unique Archetypes for your character.

Step Two: Attributes

Your Attributes describe everything that your ghoul is. When you see a weight lifter on television, the adjectives that you might use to describe him would be Traits used in **Mind's Eye Theatre** roleplaying. You could say that he was *Brawny*, *Burly* or *Tough*. A suave soap opera star might be described as *Alluring*, *Charming* or *Gorgeous*. In **Mind's Eye Theatre**, all of these things become Traits that your character possesses.

From the list of Attributes in **Laws of the Night**, decide which ones best describe your character. Attributes fall into three categories: Physical, Mental and Social. You need to pick one of these three as your Primary and assign seven Traits to it. The one next in importance is Secondary; give this category five Traits. The remaining one is Tertiary, which receives three Traits.

Let your character inspiration determine your Attributes. If your ghoul is a bodyguard for the Ventrue primogen, making Physical Attributes his weakest area would not be wise. You may take a Trait more than once if you want to reflect a greater level of aptitude in a particular area. For example, the aforementioned power lifter might have *Brawny* x 5.

Step Three: Advantages

Choosing Abilities

Abilities are the skills your character has picked up in life. Whether your ghoul learned to fight, perform surgery or write poetry, all of these Abilities may come into play during a story. Each Ability allows you to perform a specialized task, and on occasion Ability Traits can be bid instead of Attributes. Choose five Traits from the complete list on page 23 of **Laws of the Night**. Additional, ghoul-specific Abilities can be found in this book on page 41.

Disciplines

Ghouls must choose their initial Discipline from among the so-called Physical Disciplines. If you take Negative Traits or Flaws, these points may

be used to buy other Disciplines, but only if you also take the Merit: *Learn Other Disciplines*. You can find a complete description of Disciplines starting on page 75 of **Laws of the Night**.

Choosing Influences

Influences represent the control you exert over the World of Darkness. These are the subtle player's bread and butter. If Brujah punks give you trouble, they might learn their lesson when you spend enough *Police* Influences to have their haven raided at 10:30 A.M. You may take three Influences during character creation. Your choices are listed in **Laws of the Night**, starting on page 29. These Influences may be the reason you were made into a ghoul, the things that your Regnant puts you in charge of, or may simply be things you have acquired on your own.

Choosing Humanity Traits

The last part of the Advantages stage is selecting your three Humanity Traits from the list in the Humanity section on page **36** of this book. These represent your ties to your human side that oppose the Beast within you.

Step Four: Last Touches

You may now more fully define your character by taking up to four Negative Traits. This step is completely optional, but does allow you to take additional positive Traits, Influences and Humanity Traits on a one-for-one basis. Purchasing Numina costs two Negative Traits per level of Numina.

Now is the time to record your four Blood Traits and one Willpower Trait on your character sheet.

You may also take up to five Traits' worth of Flaws and five of Merits, assuming your character concept supports them. In other words, a ghoul with the Flaw: *Low Pain Threshold* probably doesn't have several facial piercings.

If it's in character, you can also take Derangements. They provide extra points to spend. For each Derangement that you take, you receive two additional Traits to spend on your character. Revenants are required take one Derangement during character creation, but do not receive extra Traits from it.

Sample Character Creation

Gina has been playing a Ventrue for a while, and wants a break. She would like to bring in a new character, and her Storyteller suggests a ghoul.

She comes up with the foundation of her ghoul character. Her ghoul is a blues singer, Blood Bound to a Gangrel who's just entered the city. The Storyteller checks with the Gangrel's player, who agrees to it, and it's off to the races.

First, Gina comes up with a name. Flipping through the paper, she comes across the name "Jimenez." She likes the sound of it, and looks for a first name in a baby-name book. "Maya" has a nice ring to it and fits harmoniously with her chosen surname. Now that Maya has a name, Gina thinks about who Maya actually is.

Her deliberation determines that Maya was a singer in roadside clubs when she caught the attention of a traveling Gangrel named Kekkova Romanovich, who was looking for some companionship on the road. Backstage, Kekkova made her offer to Maya, who, tired of playing the same one-horse towns, accepted. The two have been together ever since, with Maya doing Kekkova's legwork and scouting out potential victims.

The back story makes sense to both the Storyteller and Kekkova's player, so it's on to Traits. While Maya comes across as something of a dreamer, she's happiest when she has her own space, something that Kekkova respects. Gina chooses the Nature and Demeanor, Loner and Visionary, respectively. Next, Gina ranks Mental, Social and Physical Traits in that order, and picks the specific Traits that suit her concept of a tough-but-attractive singer who has managed to survive on her own in a very nasty world.

Picking Attributes

Gina chooses the Mental Traits *Cunning*, *Shrewd* and a couple of levels of *Wily* right off the bat. She decides that these are useful in contract negotiations and dealings with promoters and booking agents. *Attentive* and *Vigilant* are added, which have enabled Maya to spot trouble and duck it. Finally, Gina tacks on *Clever*, just on general principle. Maya may not have had much education, but that doesn't mean she's dumb.

Next come Social Traits. Gina starts with *Eloquent*, as a reflection of Maya's talent for writing lyrics. Then it's on to what Traits might make up the singer's stage persona: *Beguiling*, *Dignified*, *Gorgeous* and *Seductive*.

Last but not least are Physical Traits. Gina already knows that Maya is better at running than fighting, and holds to the philosophy that the safest place to be in a fight is far away from it. She therefore picks the Traits *Dexterous* (x 2) and *Quick*.

Humanity comes next, and Gina decides that Maya's actually something of a softy. Gina determines that Maya is *Generous* and *Empathetic*, but also *Loyal* to Kekkova.

Sample Character

Physical Traits

Dexterous x 2
Quick

Social Traits

Beguiling Seductive
Dignified
Eloquent
Gorgeous

Mental Traits

Attentive
Cunning, Clever
Shrewd, Vigilant
Wily x 2

Negative Traits

Delicate

Abilities

Performance (Singing) x 3
Kindred Lore
Masquerade

Disciplines

Alacrity

Backgrounds

Status
Recognized

Merits

Learn Other
Disciplines
(3 Trait Merit)

Flaws

Insomnia
(2 Trait Flaw)

Humanity

Loyal, Generous,
Empathetic

Willpower

○ ○ ○ ○ ○ ○ ○ ○ ○ ○
□ □ □ □ □ □ □ □ □ □

Blood

○ ○ ○ ○ ○ ○ ○ ○ ○ ○
■ ■ ■ ■ □ □ □ □ □ □

Influences

Transportation x 3

Derangements

None

Liber des Goules

The Book of Ghouls

Player _____ Gina DeBarthe

Character _____ Maya Jimenez

Chronicle _____ Daylight Madness

Nature _____ Loner

Demeanor _____ Visionary

Concept _____ Traveling Performer

Regnant _____ Kekkova Romanovich

Regnant's Clan _____ Gangrel

Haven _____ With Kekkova

Experience _____

Then come Abilities. Three Traits' worth of *Performance* is a must. *Masquerade* and *Kindred Lore* seem natural as well, because Maya and Kekkova spend considerable time together on the road.

Gina chooses the *Celerity* Discipline; Maya's much more into flight than fight.

Maya's only Status Trait is *Recognized*, so she marks it down and moves on. As for Influences, knowing the ins and outs of *Transportation* (x 3) seems appropriate, since Maya and Kekkova travel a lot. All ghouls start with four Blood Traits, so Gina puts those down along with a single Willpower Trait.

Basic character creation is done at this point, but Gina wants some maneuverability points-wise. She gives her ghoul the Negative Trait: *Delicate*. Gina also wants Maya to be able to learn other Disciplines over time, so she gives her the Merit: *Learn Other Disciplines*. Combined with her Negative Trait, this puts her two Traits in the hole. The balance will have to be made up somehow. Gina chooses the two-trait Flaw: *Insomnia*.

Satisfied, Gina sits down to flesh out the details of Maya's pre-ghoul existence. This record, as well as her character sheet, is shown to a Storyteller before game time for approval. When play begins, Kekkova is "reunited" with her favorite ghoul.

The Becoming

I don't like your tragic sighs,
as if your god has passed you by.
Well, hey fool, that's your deception.
— Sarah McLachlan, "Ice"

Making Mortal Characters into Ghouls

In a **Mind's Eye Theatre** game, new mortals who catch a vampire's eye can expect to be ghouled. The transformation from normal human to ghoul begins with the introduction of vampire blood, one Blood Trait's worth, into the mortal's system. The vitae must somehow *enter* the body of the intended ghoul, whether orally or intravenously, or else it has no effect. Topical applications of vitae are inevitably failures (not even pouring vampire blood into open wounds has a very high success rate), and are extremely humiliating to the vampires caught attempting them.

If the vampire making a ghoul has the Flaw: *Thin Blooded*, or is of 13th generation, a Static Challenge must be made to determine if the ghouling succeeds. If the vampire wins the mortal becomes a ghoul (would-be creators with *Thin Blooded* lose all ties). Ghouls created by *Thin Blooded* vampires acquire the same Flaw. Otherwise the mortal character becomes a perfectly "healthy" ghoul.

A mortal character acquires a few things immediately upon becoming a ghoul. The first is the Blood Trait that her creator injects into her system. The second is an additional Trait in her Primary Attribute category. This Trait, as well as any Disciplines learned, is lost should the character ever return to full mortal status.

On the other hand, each new ghoul loses a Humanity Trait instantly. This Trait is gone forever. It will not automatically return if the ghoul rejoins the mass of humankind.

Humanity

A man feared he might find an assassin;
Another that he might find a victim.
One was more wise than the other.
— Stephen Crane

Humanity is one of the most important parts of a ghoul's being. It describes how close a ghoul is to his human nature. Conversely, it is also a measure of how thoroughly a ghoul has been sucked into his Regnant's culture. Humans normally start out with four Humanity Traits, and can ascend to a total of eight. Most ghouls start out with three (one is lost when the blood is taken). Revenants start with one Humanity Trait, and may never obtain more than four (only Grimaldi ghouls may get this far; members of the other families are restricted to one). Revenants' existence is so essentially inhuman that it is impossible for them to empathize fully with normal people. While humans and other ghouls can never lose their last Humanity Trait, Revenants can and often do.

Humanity Traits

Benevolent, Charitable, Chivalrous, Empathetic, Fair, Generous, Giving, Gracious, Helpful, Honorable, Humane, Innocent, Kind, Liberal, Loyal, Merciful, Moral, Naive, Pious, Sympathetic and *Warm.*

Capitalist society at large deems the equivalent of Humanity Traits to be disadvantages. Loyalty keeps you on the low end of the corporate ladder, sympathy gets you mugged, and you can't afford to be merciful. Machiavelli's Prince is the golden idol of our age, and vampires emulate this ideal to a frightening degree. Ghouls, as reflections of vampires, may attempt to shed their Humanity to emulate their masters. But, believe it or not, Humanity does have its benefits.

Using Humanity

The uses of Humanity Traits are varied. Not only can they be used to power Numina (as stated in **Antagonists**), they can be used in other situations.

• **Relief from Derangements** — A ghoul player can spend one Humanity Trait in the presence of a Storyteller early in gameplay to relieve her character of a fear-related Derangement for the duration of that evening's play. Derangements triggered by *Chimerstry* or *Obtenebration* are affected by this use of Humanity, while *Presence*-spawned terrors are not.

This sort of expenditure of Humanity Traits should be played out. Whether a character confides in a trusted friend about his constant battle to work through a Derangement, prays vociferously for strength, or displays the St. Christopher medal that his mother gave him on her deathbed, there should be some in-game action to demonstrate the expenditure of this very important Trait.

• **Threats to Life and Limb** — Humanity Traits can also be used when a character's "fight or flight" instinct is triggered. In a survival situation, a player can spend a Humanity Trait and add one to the Traits being put to the test. This only works in life-threatening situations.

• **True Love** — Assuming a ghoul has a True Love (Storytellers should know about this sort of thing in advance; making up the light of your life on the spot tends to stretch credulity a bit), a Humanity Trait can be used as it is for Threats to Life and Limb if the loved one is in mortal danger.

Similarly, a Humanity Trait can be used in place of a regular Trait during a character's initial bid if his loved one is at risk during the challenge. This is quite useful, particularly if the character no longer has an appropriate Trait to bid but is compelled to act anyway. A Humanity Trait used in this way is lost, regardless of the outcome of the challenge.

Losing Humanity

If a ghoul enters a frenzy and harms or kills someone, a check must be made to see if the character loses a Humanity Trait. (If no one is hurt, the ghoul suffers no long-term scars from the frenzy.) If someone is indeed injured as a result of a ghoul's frenzy, the ghoul must win a Static Social Challenge against four Traits. If the ghoul wins the challenge, he is unaffected by his experience and maintains all Humanity. If the ghoul loses, he acquires a Derangement (to be determined by the Storyteller). He also loses a Humanity Trait, though not permanently.

In the event that the ghoul kills someone during frenzy, accidentally or otherwise, an immediate challenge must be made against a Storyteller or Narrator. This takes the form of two Static Challenges, for which the ghoul must bid a Humanity Trait. Loss of one challenge or a tie in both temporarily

costs the Trait that was bid and gives the ghoul a Derangement (Storyteller choice). If the ghoul ties one test and loses the other, or loses both, he permanently loses the Humanity Trait he bid and acquires a Derangement.

A ghoul can only *permanently* lose a Humanity Trait from frenzying if he kills someone. (This heinous act lowers the character's maximum Humanity by one Trait.) Under no other circumstances can a character lose Humanity permanently (allowing for Storyteller discretion — an exception can be made in the case of torturers, vivisectors and the like). Humanity Traits lost *temporarily* can be regained with experience and good roleplaying. Humanity Traits that are permanently lost cannot be restored under any normal circumstances.

Of course, if a ghoul kills someone during frenzy but both of his Static Challenges are successes, he loses no Humanity Traits and doesn't gain any Derangements.

For Example

Dana's character has a maximum of seven Humanity Traits. At the moment she only has six (the result of using one earlier in the evening). However, she has just killed an innocent bystander while in the throes of a Frenzy. She immediately finds a Storyteller and tells him what happened.

The Storyteller conducts the mandatory Humanity check. Dana announces that she's bidding her Humanity Trait *Innocent*; this will serve as the bid *for both challenges.* In the first challenge, the Storyteller comes up Rock while Dana comes up Scissors. The second attempt finds both Storyteller and Dana with Rock. Dana loses one challenge and ties the other, so permanently loses *Innocent*, a Trait that she can never regain. In addition, the Storyteller assigns Dana the Derangement: *Undying Remorse*, because her character is so concerned with keeping her Humanity.

From here on, Dana can only have a maximum of six Humanity Traits. Her innocence (not to mention her *Innocent*) is lost forever.

Frenzies aren't the only way to lose Humanity. Acts of outrageous or unnecessary cruelty, crimes or other immoral acts can all lead to the leaching of a ghoul's Humanity. On the following page is a chart of some actions that can lead to Humanity loss, and the penalties associated with them.

Scale of Wrongdoing, Challenges and Penalties

Crime	Challenge	Potential Penalty
Purposely inflicting injury	Static vs. 4 Soc.	Loss of Humanity Trait bid, can be bought back with experience points.
Theft and robbery	Static vs. 5 Soc.	Loss of Humanity Trait bid, can be bought back with experience points.
Unreasoning destruction	Static vs. 6 Soc.	Loss of Humanity Trait bid, can be bought back with experience points.
Accidental killing	2 Static	Loss of one challenge or tie of both; loss of Humanity Trait bid (to be gained back with experience), and gain Derangement of Storyteller choice. Loss of one challenge and one tie, or loss of both; permanent loss of Humanity Trait bid, and gain Derangement of Storyteller choice.
Premeditated murder	2 Static vs. 6 Soc.	Loss of either challenge results in permanent loss of Humanity Trait bid and gain of one Derangement of Storyteller choice. Humanity Traits cannot exceed six afterward.
Mass murder, torture	3 Static vs. 9 Soc.	Loss of even one challenge results in the permanent loss of two Humanity Traits and the gain of two Derangements, both Storyteller choice. Humanity Traits lost are permanent, subtracted from current maximum of Humanity Traits available to the character.

Roleplaying

Remember, losing Humanity is a terrible thing. The erosion of a ghoul's soul profoundly affects the character's personality. The more Humanity a ghoul loses, the closer she comes to her Regnant's Beast, the harder it becomes for her to break her Bond, the more she retreats from human society and the less useful she becomes to her Regnant. Characters who lose Humanity tend to be cynical, jaded and vicious; the loss of even one Trait can have a noticeable effect on long-established behavior patterns.

Regaining Humanity

Regaining Humanity Traits depends on how you lost them. Humanity spent to power Numina, save a loved one, counteract a fear, or face a life-threatening situation can be regained in time (in other words, by the next event all Traits spent this way return). Ghouls who are in a hurry or in desperate need can also spend a Willpower Trait to regain a Humanity Trait.

Humanity Traits lost in a Humanity test may be bought back with experience points (to the ghoul's current rating), unless those Traits were lost permanently. Humanity Traits lost permanently can only be regained through extraordinary penance, decreed by a Storyteller and roleplayed out over a series of sessions. Humanity lost should never be returned lightly.

Storytellers should take note of characters who constantly lose and regain Humanity Traits. If this situation becomes chronic, the Storyteller may declare that the character has become jaded, and may no longer attempt to regain Humanity Traits that have been lost.

Abilities

The Abilities in this section are either new or restated from previous books to suit the lifestyle and needs of a ghoul. They can be used by any sort of ghoul, whether Hunter, Servitor or revenant. Ghouls may take these Abilities multiple times to demonstrate increased expertise. Thus, a ghoul with *Steward* x 1 may be able to run his Regnant's haven for a night or two, but a ghoul with *Steward* x 4 could fend off all manner of outside threats to his sleeping Regnant by using the haven's defenses to their utmost potential.

Animal Affinity

Animal Affinity describes how well a ghoul relates to normal, nonghoul animals. In addition to making the ghoul with this Ability inoffensive to animals (*a la Animalism*), the Ability imparts a degree of empathy with the animal condition. Ghouls who train animals should not be without *Animal Affinity*.

Animal Affinity also grants some small measure of control over creatures. When a ghoul with *Animal Affinity* makes a command or request of an animal, the creature must make a Mental Challenge to understand and carry out the order. As with *Animal Ken*, the difficulty of the test is based on the animal's level of domestication and the complexity of the task.

The character need only make a Static Challenge to calm an injured, attacking or frightened animal.

Blood Lore

This Ability indicates your knowledge of the Blood Bond. You know that you are Bound, you know that your feelings for your Regnant are false, and you may have some idea of how to break the Bond. Ghouls with this Ability have the potential to destroy the unlives of their Regnants. To learn this Ability, speak with your Storyteller to see if it is appropriate for your character.

Haven Scouting

This Ability is invaluable to both Servitors and Hunters. This is the capacity to find a new haven for your Regnant if he needs one fast, or to sniff out likely places where a vampire might have gone to ground for the day. Almost all applications of *Haven Scouting* require Mental Challenges, with the difficulty determined by either the ghoul's time remaining before dawn or his familiarity with his quarry.

Hunter Lore

Closely related to *Lupine Lore*, this shows your knowledge of different types of Hunters (and not just ghouled ones), their reputations and some of their tactics. This can help you protect your Regnant or yourself. Gaining

information on a Hunter works in the same way that it does for *Lupine Lore*. However, researching a Hunter's tactics or abilities requires a Mental Challenge. Obviously the difficulty of the challenge depends on the type of information being sought.

Kindred Lore

This is your familiarity with your Regnant's lineage and the mysteries shrouding her unnatural evolution. This Ability can aid you greatly in either blackmailing your Regnant or sweet-talking her into cutting you a little slack. In addition, this Ability gives you accurate information on what does and doesn't kill vampires, enabling you to separate fact from myth.

Lupine Lore

Well, you know there are vampires out there, so why not believe in werewolves, too? You know they're in the woods, you may know how much they hate vampires, and you definitely know how much vampires hate them. With enough experience invested in this Ability, you may even discover where the local Lupine pack hangs out. The use of this Ability requires a Social Challenge with the difficulty directly affected by the Rank and Renown of the werewolf in question, or by the relative secrecy of the meeting place.

Masquerade

This Ability can be a real icebreaker at parties, though not always a good one unless you're in with a gaggle of good-humored Malkavians. This Ability allows you to pass for a vampire — an especially useful skill for a Hunter. There's nothing like being able to walk into a city and be presented to the prince, particularly when you intend to jam a sharpened croquet post through his wishbone.

This Ability allows a single re-test on *Aura Perceptions* performed against ghouls who possess it. It does not, however, fool the Garou Gift: *Sense Wyrm*.

Medical Knowledge

You know a great deal about medical procedures, just as the name suggests. This Ability can be invaluable to a ghoul, as the mostly living have only limited use of blood to heal their wounds. *Medical Knowledge* also allows a character to perform medical procedures on other ghouls and living creatures with similar physiologies (humans — yes; Garou in Crinos form — no). This can halt a bleeding character's decline of Health Levels, or stabilize a Dying character at Incapacitated. Multiple Traits of *Medical Knowledge* allow a character to stabilize a Dying character for up to an hour before she needs to go to a hospital.

To accomplish any of these feats, a ghoul must make a Static Mental Challenge against six Traits. The challenge should become more difficult according to the number and severity of injuries the ghoul is attempting to heal.

Medical Knowledge can also be extended to other uses. Ghouls with this Ability can assess the effects of drugs and dosages, ascertain causes of death, diagnose diseases and otherwise put their knowledge of how human anatomy works to good use.

Sniping

Ghouls with this Ability are so in tune with vampires that they can pick one out in a crowd. They can instinctively spot the predator. Working almost like a psychic power, this is really more of a subconscious assessment of the hallmarks of vampires.

Sniping basically grants a ghoul a very specific sort of *Aura Perception*. By using *Sniping*, a ghoul can enter a Social Challenge with a single target. If the ghoul wins, he may ask if his target is a vampire or not. The target cannot lie in response to this question, and even *Mask of 1000 Faces* cannot hide a vampire from a talented ghoul who knows *Sniping*.

Steward

Every vampire should be so lucky or intelligent as to have a ghoul with this Ability. *Steward* demonstrates a ghoul's grasp of his Regnant's affairs, day- or nighttime. A ghoul with this Ability can run every aspect of his Regnant's haven. This Ability is useful for defending the haven against invaders, but it can also be brought to bear should a ghoul decide to defect from his Regnant's service. Not only is a good *Steward* fully stocked with blackmail material on his Regnant, but he just might know her haven better than she does.

Blood Use

For the blood is the life.

— Deuteronomy, 12:23

Unlike mortals, ghouls begin play with four Blood Traits. This includes the three normal ones that humans have, plus one Trait's worth of vampiric blood. Ghouls can actually have up to six Blood Traits (three human, three vampiric) in their systems at any given time, but any more causes harm at the rate of one Health Level per additional Blood Trait.

Unlike vampires, ghouls do not need blood to exist, save for those ghouls who have exceeded what their natural life spans would have been. Ghouls can use blood to heal, though only nonaggravated wounds. Aggravated damage, caused by things such as fire, Garou claws and teeth, vampire fangs and claws,

or weapons treated with blood from Quietus, can only be healed with the passage of time.

Ghouls are a bit more fragile than vampires, however, and ghouls who are down by two or more Health Levels are in serious danger. In addition, a ghoul who empties his Blood Pool must win a Static Challenge against six Physical Traits or die from blood loss. If the ghoul wins, enough vampire blood remains in his system to allow him to cling to life, however feebly.

Health

A sound mind in a sound body, is a short but full description of a happy state in this world.

— John Locke, *Some Thoughts Concerning Education*

As ghouls are still to some extent human, Health Levels work differently for them than for vampires. For a ghoul, the four Health Levels below Healthy are Bruised, Wounded, Incapacitated and Dying. There is no Torpor for a ghoul; once her heart stops she is dead. An Incapacitated ghoul is not unconscious, however. She simply may not engage in any challenges, and is completely at the mercy of those around her.

As their hearts still pump, ghouls also have the unfortunate problem of bleeding when wounded. A ghoul who is Wounded will, after 10 minutes without medical attention, lose a Blood Trait and slip down to Incapacitated. An Incapacitated ghoul, if not treated within 10 minutes, will lose another Blood Trait and slip down to Dying. Dying ghouls will lose a Blood Trait every 10 minutes until they are tapped out; at this point death is the likely result.

The only other one is the Embrace, but players are advised not to count on this sort of rescue.

Bleeding can be stopped with a minimum of medical attention. Any character with medicine-related Abilities can tend to an injured ghoul and stop the downward spiral of blood loss. The character does this by announcing that she is attempting to stop the bleeding, and then by winning or tying a Static Mental Challenge. However, a ghoul who is bleeding to death and is already Incapacitated (or worse) cannot treat herself. As the ghoul cannot participate in a challenge, it is impossible for her to perform the Static Mental Challenge and stop her own bleeding.

Bleeding from aggravated wounds can also be stopped in this manner, but the structural damage caused by the wound can only be healed with intense medical attention (read: hospitalization). Ghouls heal one Level of aggravated damage per game session *if they spend their downtime receiving medical care.* Otherwise, Storyteller discretion is advised.

Aging

Age doth not rectify, but incurvate our natures, turning bad dispositions into worser habits.

— Sir Thomas Browne, *Religio Medici*

The revenant families aside, ghouldom is not a permanent state. Ghouls will revert to true humanity after 30 days without a Trait's worth of vampire blood. This time limit is absolute, and the switchover is instantaneous. A ghoul who reverts to her mortal state loses any additional Traits related to her ghouling, not to mention all of her Disciplines. If she becomes a ghoul again, the Traits are returned but the highest level attained in each Discipline is lost (you always retain the most basic level of any Discipline, though). Nor are lost Humanity Traits regained; the character has seen too much to return to innocence.

In addition, vampire blood keeps ghouls young. If a ghoul with under a hundred years of service stops receiving vitae, he begins to age normally from that point onward. Ghouls who have been in their current states for more than a century face a slightly different problem. These old-timers begin to age at an advanced rate, effectively 10 or more times normal. In game terms, for every hour past deadline, an aged ex-ghoul must win a Static Physical Challenge against 10 Traits. If she ties or loses, she drops one Health Level (though without bleeding), loses a Physical Trait and gains a Negative Physical Trait (Storyteller's choice). The Trait changes are permanent, even if the character does later manage to acquire vampire blood again.

Characters who lose and regain their not-quite-human status cease to age the moment they become ghouls again. The restored ghouls do not grow more youthful with new infusions of vitae. A ghoul's existence is a holding action against time, and nothing more.

If a character, against all logic, somehow manages to keep poking along without vampire blood for an extended period of time, Storytellers should feel free to intercede and help nature take its course.

Another Vampire Trait

One of the more remarkable things about ghouls is their ability to frenzy. Ghoul frenzies are more rare than their vampiric counterparts, usually only occurring when a ghoul faces imminent destruction. However, when Humanity fails, the Beast, the overwhelming desire to survive, takes over. frenzies can also be brought on by incredible amounts of stress, triggered Derangements or by the *Animalism* Discipline.

When a ghoul is in a situation in which her Humanity cannot help her escape, and all of her Willpower is gone, she may declare that she is in frenzy. Ghoul Frenzy works much like vampiric frenzy. The ghoul becomes violent and attacks blindly in desperate need to escape. While in frenzy, a ghoul may ignore damage penalties to the point of death, but she cannot use blood to heal and is still susceptible to blood loss. Any damage done to a ghoul past Dying will kill her.

Derangements can also trigger frenzy in a ghoul. A ghoul under the influence of her Derangement(s), or who is being pressured about them by another character, may slide into a frenzy as a form of self-defense. In this case, the ghoul makes a Static Mental Challenge against 10 Traits. If she ties or fails, she goes into frenzy.

Ghouls do not gain Beast Traits from frenzying. If a ghoul commits a heinous act while frenzying, a check must be made to see if the character loses a Humanity Trait. However, if the frenzy passes without anything untoward happening, there is no need to check for Humanity loss.

The Blood Bond

When love is repressed, hate takes its place.
— Havelock Ellis, *On Life and Sex: Essays of Love and Virtue*

The third time is a charm when it comes to ingesting vampire blood; that's how many sips it takes to Blood Bond someone. The Bond is henceforth at the absolute center of a ghoul's life. The more thoroughly he is tied to his Regnant, the more perfect his Regnant will appear to him and the more important (or pleasurable) serving her becomes. As the Bond strengthens, the ghoul finds himself excusing his Regnant's flaws, rationalizing her tyrannical behavior, and generally surrendering to the overwhelming emotional impact of the vitae.

Of course, a ghoul is still human, and may know or guess that his feelings are coerced. However, this is not sufficient impetus to allow a ghoul to break the Bond. Think about it this way: Lovers have their quarrels, and best friends can become disgusted with their counterparts' actions, but in most cases they are apt to forgive or withhold judgment because it's their lover or best friend. It works the same way with the Bond.

Bound ghouls are easier to Dominate and coerce than are unbound ghouls, or even normal humans. Once a vampire has Bound a ghoul to her, she need no longer make eye contact to use Dominate on the hapless Thrall. In addition, in any contests between Regnant and Thrall the vampire wins all ties. However, these effects are Regnant-specific; a ghoul Bound to the local Tremere elder won't necessarily be easy for another Ventrue to Dominate.

The saving grace that ghouls have in their Blood Bonds is the fact that their still-human metabolisms produce plenty of fresh, untainted blood with which to replenish their systems. If a Regnant doesn't feed a Bound ghoul at least once a year, the Bond will fade.

Breaking the Bond

The more violent the love, the more violent the anger.
— Burmese proverb

The ease of breaking from a Bond often has to do with an individual ghoul's Derangements and Nature. A Loner has a much better chance of breaking his chains than does a Sycophant. Meanwhile, someone who slips into childlike behavior during Derangement spells may cling to her Regnant as a child might an abusive parent.

There are no set rules for breaking a Blood Bond; each ghoul must decide for herself how to become free. Most ghouls, unless mistreated severely, won't want to break their Bonds. Also consider that a Bound ghoul has a steady source of vitae; ghouls on the loose don't necessarily know where their next metaphysical meals are coming from. Only drastic behavior on the part of a Regnant should motivate a ghoul to contemplate freedom.

If a ghoul character has a sadistic or cruel Regnant (providing, of course, that the ghoul doesn't like that kind of treatment), the player should keep a Storyteller informed of what's going on. In time, and with Storyteller permission, the ghoul may be able to break free of the vampire's influence. The escape will not be easy. In fact it should be the single-most-difficult thing the character experiences in the course of the game. There is a great emotional struggle between the imposed love of the Bond and the character's own sense of self. Most ghouls are incapable of winning that battle.

Time can also sever the Bond, but a year without blood will almost certainly kill old ghouls; the process calls for caution and a backup source of vitae. In addition, without vitae, a ghoul is just a normal human being and, in many cases, a target. Vampirism, like murder, should have no witnesses, and a ghoul who walks away from the Bond is a threat to the Masquerade.

Embracing a Ghoul

Even as love crowns you shall he crucify you,
even as he is for your growth so is he for your pruning.
— Kahlil Gibran, *The Prophet*

Sometimes the creation of a ghoul is the equivalent of a test drive for a vampire. Creating a ghoul enables him to see how well a potential childe might work out. Would-be sires can keep an eye on their ghoul prospects and come to decisions at their leisure. A ghoul character who is observed in this fashion could remain a ghoul for any length of time, ranging from a month to a decade to forever if the vampire decides that she is unsuitable for elevation. On the other hand, there are those vampires who kill their failed would-be progeny. The possible reward in a situation like this is great, but so is the risk.

If a Regnant decides to take a drastic step with her ghoul and Embrace him, the process functions largely like the Embrace of a mortal. Embraced ghouls retain all of their previously learned Disciplines, and acquire those Traits that go into making a vampire. They do, however, lose all of their Humanity Traits and any Numina they might have possessed.

(**Note:** Ghouls who are Embraced do not receive a complete set of new Disciplines on top of the ones they already possess. Instead, those Disciplines already learned go toward rounding out the new vampire's initial allotment.)

Willpower

The good or ill of man lies within his own will.

— Epictetus, *Discourses*

In times of desperation and strife, people have been known to do things that would normally be impossible. These superhuman efforts are said to be the product of chemistry, but in the World of Darkness this capacity is represented by Willpower. One of a ghoul's few weapons against the encroaching inhumanity of the World of Darkness, Willpower wraps up her desire to live and her sense of self into a single package. It is what makes Bonding ghouls necessary, and also makes it possible to throw off the Blood Bond.

Ghouls start with a single Willpower Trait. Later, they can buy up to six during the course of the game. Willpower Traits can be used for multiple things:

• A ghoul can spend a Willpower Trait to negate instances of frenzy.

• Willpower can bring a ghoul back up to full in one Attribute category (Physical, Mental or Social).

• Willpower can also be used to ignore the effects of any wounds, up to and including Incapacitation, for the duration of one challenge. However, no application of Willpower is capable of healing a character.

• A Willpower Trait can be spent to stave off incipient death for 15 minutes, assuming nothing else is done to send the character further on his way to the grave.

• A Willpower Trait can be expended to ignore the effects of any one Mental or Social Challenge, including ones from a ghoul's Regnant, *if and only if* the effects of the challenge would cause the ghoul to perform an action that would be deeply at odds with her Nature or personal ethics.

Keep in mind that once a Willpower Trait is gone, it is unavailable until the end of a story. At that time, a ghoul regains all the Willpower he used. A Narrator or Storyteller can grant Willpower more frequently to players who exhibit exceptional roleplaying or great improvement in their roleplaying style, but such rewards should be handed out infrequently at best.

Ghoul Merits and Flaws

The sunshine, too light, the ocean too wide,
I'm sick of your cliché,
The sky is kind, love is blind,
You can't let go of the lost pain.
— Cibo Matto, " Le Pain Perdu"

Psychological

Aware of False Love: (2 Trait Merit)

Ghouls possessing this Merit are aware of the nature of the Blood Bond. They know that what they feel for their Regnants is not natural, and are therefore more capable when dealing with their feelings.

If you have this Merit, your Regnant is two Traits down when attempting to coerce or *Dominate* you in any way.

Cannibalism: (3 Trait Flaw)

The first taste of your Regnant's blood turned you on to the taste of raw flesh. Now you think that *human tartare* is the only way to go. This Flaw can get so demanding that you might scour the streets for the "other" white meat. The whole thing becomes a brutal obsession, and you settle for nothing less than the taste of human. Cows, pigs, chickens — they're all safe from you. It's *homo sapiens a la mode* that satisfies your craving, and if you can't get a fix you just might go mad….

Ostentatious Toady: (3 Trait Flaw)

You have thrived since your Regnant first gave you her blood. The power she grants you is apparent in your unnatural strength, toughness and speed. The only problem (and you'd never admit it) is the fact that you know you would be nothing without the blood. Your Regnant is the only thing that makes you truly alive. As a result, you constantly try to impress her, even if the attempt means risking your life. You must spend a Willpower Trait whenever you're faced with a particularly juicy chance to show off for your Regnant. For example, if your Regnant mentions that she wishes for a pompous Ventrue primogen to be run over with a steamroller, you might dial up construction-equipment companies and inquire about rentals.

Squeamish: (2 Trait Flaw)

When your Regnant first made you into a ghoul, you were nearly ill. How could she make you drink her blood? You can't deny the tremendous advantages that her vitae (*That sounds better now, doesn't it? We'll call it vitae, and that way we can pretend it's not blood.*) has provided, but you must spend a Willpower Trait every time you drink. If faced with a gruesome scene (combat doesn't count, unless people are really messy), you must either leave immediately or win a Static Challenge to bear the sight of the gore. If the challenge is lost, you may still stay, but feel extremely ill. To reflect this queasiness, you lose two Physical Traits (you can regain them with one Willpower Trait) and gain the Negative Trait: *Witless* for the duration of the scene.

Swept Away: (2 Trait Flaw)

Ah, the beauty of it all! After you got over the initial shock of your Regnant's true nature, you were enthralled by the romance and heartbreaking tragedy of vampirism. You are needed, loved, provided for — how wonderful!

A ghoul who is *Swept Away* basically blinds himself to the nature of his relationship with his Regnant. His master may be cruel or abusive, but in the end it doesn't matter. The ghoul sees her only through rose-colored glasses. A character with this Flaw is down two Traits when his Regnant attempts to *Dominate* him.

Mental

Insomnia: (2 Trait Flaw)

Try as you might, much-needed sleep never comes to you. This problem has been nagging at you since the trauma of your first taste of vitae, and the falling of the scales from your eyes. The best you can manage is a fitful hour of dozing or a catnap here or there. It wouldn't be so bad if you didn't need the rest so badly — lack of sleep is just wearing you down.

To reflect the effects of your affliction, you start every event at full Traits. At the halfway point of the game, however, your current Mental, Physical and Social Trait ratings all decrease by one.

Well Rested: (1 Trait Merit)

You need very little sleep. As few as three hours out of a full 24 will normally let you wake up brighteyed and bushytailed (so to speak). This can greatly aid your Regnant by allowing you to help her all night and for part of the day, as well as allowing you to live your own life.

Supernatural

Animal Friendship: (2 Trait Merit)

Not only do animals find you inoffensive, they actively like you. You have an extraordinary rapport with animals that convinces them to come when called and occasionally aid you at your request. Of course, the animals'

exact reactions to your requests depends on their degree of domestication, native intelligence, and sense of self-preservation. This Merit works well with the *Animal Affinity* Ability.

Learn Other Disciplines: (3 Trait Merit)

You are one of the lucky few who has the ability to learn Disciplines beyond a ghoul's basic bill of fare. However, you must have a mentor to teach you these new powers. Otherwise, all the talent in the world won't help you pick up *Auspex*.

The price for each level of any new Discipline is exactly the same as if a ghoul were a vampire character buying an out-of-clan Discipline. Thus, if a ghoul were to try to learn the basic level of *Auspex* (*Heightened Senses*), she would have to hunt up a willing teacher and spend five experience points.

Note: *Protean* and *Thaumaturgy* are the only two Disciplines that may not be learned with this Merit.

Light Sensitivity: (3 Trait Flaw)

The Beast is strong in your Regnant's blood, strong enough to cause you problems in daylight. You can bear only short jaunts into the sunlit world, and even then you must cover up and wear sunglasses. Those same sunglasses must be worn indoors in well-lit spaces to avoid the excruciating pain that bright light causes you. You have no trouble with moonlight, and don't need sunglasses after sunset unless you go somewhere well lit (like a mall or a nighttime baseball game). Prolonged exposure (10 minutes) to direct sunlight causes you normal damage at the same rate at which a vampire takes aggravated damage.

Poaching Ghouls

Vampires want the best of anything, including ghouls. So if a vampire sees that another of his kind has a desirable or useful ghoul, he may decide to make that ghoul his own. This practice is called "poaching," and is frowned on by the Camarilla. Of course, the ones doing the frowning are generally the ones who have the most talented ghouls (and therefore the most desirable to poachers).

Setites make a special habit of stealing others' ghouls, but the practice is not restricted to them. It's just that poaching is easy for them to pull off.

Thin Blooded Regnant: (4 Trait Flaw)

Your Regnant has weak blood, which is both a blessing and curse. Power-wise she's closer to ghoul level than any vampire has a right to be. Unfortunately, this doesn't do you any good. You cannot spend any of your blood on Disciplines. Worse still, you need your Regnant's blood more often because it just barely sustains your immortality. If you don't have her blood every week, you run the risk of reverting back to full mortality. Other vampires will also actively seek to steal (or "poach") ghouls who have this Flaw.

Unbondable: (3 point Merit)

This Merit is the ace up many a ghoul's sleeve. You cannot be Bound and are therefore are immune to the disadvantages of the condition. However, you have to keep this a secret from your "Regnant," or he might be disinclined to retain you.

Kindred Ties

Blackmail Material: (1-3 Trait Merit)

You have somehow garnered very embarrassing information on a vampire of indeterminate Status. The Status of your victim and juiciness of the information depend on how many points you spend on the Merit and on the imagination of your Storyteller. Of course, you can always suggest something….

Clan Weakness: (3 Trait Flaw)

Perhaps your Regnant's blood is particularly potent, or maybe there's more darkness in your soul than you realized. At any rate, you have taken on the clan weakness of the vampire to whom you are Blood Bound. For example, Ventrue ghouls find they gain no benefits from the blood of any other clan, and Assamite ghouls take damage from other clans' blood.

Revenants may not take this Flaw.

Prestigous Regnant: (1 Trait Merit)

Your Regnant has or had great Status in the sect, and this has accorded you a peculiar honor. Most treat you respectfully, ghoul or not. This prestige can aid you greatly when you deal with vampires acquainted with your Regnant. As long as she's around, you're in the clear. If something were to happen to you, you can rest assured one of your Regnant's allies would take care of — or avenge — you.

Sabbat ghouls may take this Merit if they can find sufficient justification for doing so. However, situations in which *Prestigious Regnant* come into play for a Sabbat ghoul are few and far between.

Sugar Daddy: (1 Trait Merit)

A vampire is quite interested in you. Perhaps it's for the information you can provide him on your Regnant, or maybe he just likes your company. Whatever the reason, you've been pragmatic enough to keep channels to him open. If you need help, he may provide you with blood and a limited amount of other resources.

The main idea behind this Merit is survival, pure and simple. After all, in the World of Darkness, nothing is a sure thing. Your secret friend is insurance against your Regnant and other vampiric machinations.

Twisted Upbringing: (1 Trait Flaw)

Your Regnant has taught you all the wrong things about vampire society out of the goodness of her little black heart. Whether she told you that all the legends about garlic and running water are true or convinced you that she and all other vampires are extraterrestrials, the fact is that you bought it, lock, stock and barrel. These false ideas are bound to get you into trouble, and you will not believe any attempts to set you straight. Over time you can learn the truth and buy off this Flaw, but not until a Storyteller grants you permission.

World of Darkness Ties

Garou Ally: (2 Trait Merit)

Although both vampire and Garou societies frown on friendly interaction, exceptions can and do happen. That doesn't mean the local powers that be approve of such alliances; if your friendship were unmasked, the consequences could be grave for you and your furry friend. Whether you are Kinfolk or the two of you were old friends before either knew anything about the Wyrm or Caine, your friendship has held through all adversity. You have the right to call on your friend if you need help, and she has the right to call on you in return. In most cases, the Storyteller should create the allied character.

Physical

Damned Visage: (1 Trait Merit)

You have the uncanny ability to appear as one of the undead. Your skin is pale, your breathing is indiscernible, your hands are ice-cold, and your blinking appears practiced and unnatural. While you can't stop your heart from beating, you can spend a Blood Trait to slow your pulse to the point where it's not discernible. The only drawback to this Merit is the risk you run of fooling a Hunter so well that he might try to stake you. On the other hand, if somebody leaves you out to greet the sun, you can laugh all the way home.

Efficient Digestion: (3 Trait Merit)

You are able to go without vampire blood longer than most ghouls. In fact, you have experimented and found that you can go for two months without a drop of the good stuff. You also seem to benefit from the experience of feeding from your Regnant more than other ghouls do. Every two Blood Traits he gives you increases your Blood Pool by three (round fractions down).

Inefficient Digestion: (3 Trait Flaw)

You need twice as much blood as other ghouls; each Blood Trait your Regnant grants you only counts for half. If she gives you four, you only receive two. Halves are rounded down, so gulping down one Blood Trait has no effect on you whatsoever.

Low Pain Threshold: (2 Trait Flaw)

You hate pain and cannot understand how your Regnant bears biting her wrist to give you blood. You always think to yourself, "Oh, how that must hurt!" Indeed, the sympathy pain you feel ruins your enjoyment of the vitae. You don't like to see anything or anyone hurt. Most important, however, is the fact that you don't like seeing *yourself* hurt. Resistance to pain is not your *forte*, and the slightest amount of agony sends you into a panic or a fainting fit. While normal injuries do not do you any additional physical damage, the sheer psychological impact has a devastating effect. You will do anything to make pain stop, ranging from overdosing on painkillers to spilling all of your Regnant's secrets.

If you are subjected to threats of bodily harm, you gain the Negative Trait: *Submissive* for the remainder of the evening. If somebody actually attempts to hurt you, you either cower or flee in terror. If you can't get away, beg for mercy and debase yourself in any way in order to keep yourself from getting hurt. Once safely away from the person who threatened you, you do your best to never, ever be near him again, to the point of avoiding any room he occupies.

Unnatural Appearance: (2 Trait Flaw)

You are marked for life, whether your Regnant is a Tzimisce or vitae made the Beast manifest in your appearance. The unnatural aspect of your appearance could be an animal feature, an odd vampiric pallor to your skin, or even something inhuman in the way you move.

When afflicted with this Flaw, you are down two Traits in any Social Challenge concerning your appearance. In addition, working with the human population at large is nigh impossible. You must shroud yourself whenever you go out in public, and relations with your human friends must be completely broken off. Nosferatu and Gangrel ghouls may not take this Flaw if they already have the Flaw: *Clan Weakness*.

Vitae Sink: (2 Trait Flaw)

You need your Regnant's blood, and you need it often. It seems you can't go for longer than two weeks without it or you revert back to human state. If you have been a ghoul for over a century, this Flaw can be downright deadly.

Derangements

Sanity is a madness put to good uses; waking life is a dream controlled.
— George Santayana, *Interpretations of Poetry and Religion*

A ghoul's initiation into the supernatural can be severely damaging to her psyche. Vampires are legends made real, nightmares come to horrible life. The great majority of those given this burdensome insight buckle under its weight, and consequently gain mental afflictions called Derangements.

Not every ghoul or vampire begins play with a Derangement, but you may take one at character creation if it suits your ghoul's concept. If your character's Regnant is a Malkavian, your character probably starts out with at least one Derangement, and may gain more as time passes. Ghouls also face situations that induce Derangements. Just remember that most Derangements are survival mechanisms that the subconscious creates to protect the conscious from horrid reality.

Below are new Derangements for ghouls, as well as some familiar ones that have been modified for ghoul purposes. Others may be found in **Laws of the Night**, starting on page 44.

Amnesia

In highly traumatic situations, you sometimes forget who or even what you are. This typically occurs when you come face to face with your situation as a ghoul, or with the nightly reality of the World of Darkness. You could forget the details of the situation that triggered this response, or you could forget anything from the evening's events to your name or identity. When you are confronted by events or situations that threaten to remind you of your past, you may react violently, pass out or go into a catatonic state rather than let those memories rush back.

If you are in an incredibly stressful situation, you must perform a Static Mental Challenge against seven Traits. If you fail, you forget who you are and what you are doing there. Other memories can be lost at Storyteller discretion.

Blood Thirst

You crave the blood your Regnant gave you at the very beginning of your ghoulish existence. You will do anything to keep receiving it. You want what you need and then some — this once-a-month feeding schedule is for the birds. You will go to great lengths to get vitae, doing anything from lying to your Regnant about your use of blood, to actively hunting other vampires for the blood they possess. Even when you know drinking too much will cause you harm, you cannot help but pursue the intoxicating elixir. When your Regnant feeds you, you are always tempted to drink all that she has. Whenever you feed directly from your Regnant, you must test for Frenzy to avoid attempting to drain her completely.

Compulsive Lying

You were in New York with a friend once — his name isn't important — and you managed to convince this car dealer (he was pretty hard up to make a sale) to sell you his brand-new Dodge Viper for, like, a thousand dollars. What a great deal! He didn't even charge tax or have you go through the paperwork. He did all that himself. Oh, you want to see the car? Well… it's being repainted. It was this nasty shade of lime green. You say Vipers don't come in green? Well, this one was a special edition, signed by the president of the company. What was his name? Well, the signature wasn't very legible — you know how big businessmen are….

When this Derangement is triggered, you must spend Willpower to avoid 10 full minutes of prevarication. The lies that you spout can be as subtle or outrageous as you wish. However, the point is that you have a compulsive need to obscure the truth. "Lies" that are just a way of rephrasing the truth (for example, "Oh, I'd never be interested in joining your little cabal. Nope, nope, nope," while making it very clear that you are interested) are directly counter to the spirit of the Derangement, and hence are forbidden.

In other words, it's cheating. Don't do it.

Delusional Identity

When things get particularly hard to deal with, you often revert to someone you can trust to do a better job than you can. This new personality is someone efficient, someone stalwart, someone historic — like General Patton or Florence Nightingale. Don't worry if nobody believes you when you introduce yourself; nobody ever believes it when they meet a celebrity. Get the job at hand done quickly, efficiently and with enough zest to make people know it really was you who did it.

Psychological Note

Delusional Identities often derive from feelings of complete hopelessness and despair, and can reflect a ghoul's deepest terrors. In moments of stress or fear, the ghoul's real personality retreats and is replaced by an identity (with the same Traits, of course) that is based on the ghoul's concept of competence. This other self can be a historical, fictional or composite character. However, *Delusional Identities* that duplicate other characters already in gameplay are not allowed.

Dipsomania

Dipsomania is the urge to drink yourself into an absolute stupor when the going gets tough (or even mildly difficult). Such a Derangement can destroy the trust that others place in you, and limits your effectiveness in certain situations. This weakness, should it become known, could be used as a weapon against you (say, by a rival who offers you drinks to sidetrack you from an important mission). If this Derangement comes over you at an event, you are immediately affected by the Negative Trait: *Witless*.

Whether or not you are a "happy drunk," you are unsightly in this state. You stagger about, weave as you walk, and say all the wrong things. You may even tell the prince, to your Regnant's everlasting horror, what she *really* thinks of him — and have no memory of it the next morning.

Hebephrenia

The horror of the World of Darkness unveiled has shattered your perceptions of everything you once held as logical and real. This crisis has plunged you into a state of mind in which you maintain your sanity by clinging to the idea that everything going on is just in your head. Everyone you know, well, they're all characters in the little playworld your mind has created. Even your Regnant is just the lead in your mind's script. Everything she does is something you make her do, so you really don't mind doing what she asks.

Obviously your subconscious wanted her to ask you to do it. Those around you get pretty mad when you are rude to them, but it doesn't matter because they aren't real.

Hypochondria

You have noticed that since you became a ghoul, you get sick every time you face stress. The symptoms are usually limited to a headache or upset stomach, but are sometimes much worse. If at any time during an event you become upset about anything, you begin to think you are coming down with something suitably viral or nasty. In all probability you are quite healthy, but you need some kind of excuse to get sympathy from those around you. When you get "sick" you are effectively be down one Physical Trait for the rest of the event, or until your "attack" passes.

Immortal Fear

This Derangement reflects an absolute fear of becoming a vampire. You will go to great lengths to safeguard yourself from becoming one of the living dead, preferring to die permanently than become a creature cursed and feared the world over. What's more, you love the sun and everything associated with it. Any attempt by your Regnant to even broach the subject of your Embrace is met with either stony silence or panicked protestation. You may even turn and flee. Should anyone attempt to Embrace you, you must test for Frenzy.

Masochism

Sometimes things go wrong, dreadfully so. Deep down inside, you know it's all your fault. Since nobody else may necessarily know that you're responsible, you have to work out a way of keeping yourself in line. You do so by getting yourself into harmful situations, or by hanging around with people and creatures who dislike you. You deserve their abuse, it's your penance.

You even tend to injure yourself physically, but never to a degree that most people would notice. You don't want anybody to know what a terrible person you are, so you don't leave any marks. If a problem comes up and you are blamed, even falsely, apologize profusely and offer yourself up to the mercy of your accuser. Even if you're not responsible for whatever it is, odds are that karma is just catching up with you for a previous crime.

Obsession

You are obsessed with your Regnant. Nobody loves her like you do, and you are certain that you know what is best for her. Everybody else misunderstands her and seeks to hurt her, so you have to keep them all away. Her other ghouls may profess to love her, but they are false suitors. Their passion is nothing compared to your great, all-consuming love.

This dangerous Derangement can be activated by the presence of a new ghoul, or merely by anyone else taking an interest in your Regnant. You would rather die (taking her with you, of course) than let her be with another.

Panzaism

Since your induction into the ways and world of the vampire, you have become completely detached. When the Derangement is at its mildest, you have some trouble with the idea of the world at large being real. In a way, you seem to be halfway out of your body, simply watching events flow by. Your body may act, but it all seems so mechanical, so contrived.

When this Derangement is at its worst, things get really interesting. You "realize" that nothing is real. Nothing. You are nothing. The vampires are nothing. Everything is unreal. You can't affect the universe and the universe can't affect you because *there is nothing there*. When everything seems to be going wrong, you wrap yourself up in this mental cocoon and refuse come out until things are more to your liking.

Power Madness

You are obsessed with control, especially the idea of controlling your Regnant's affairs. When this Derangement is active, you are so preoccupied with your megalomaniacal obsessions that you lose all control of yourself. When your goals are thwarted, you come unglued and attack, either physically or verbally, those who oppose you. In short, you seek total and absolute control of your Regnant and her household.

This Derangement can also be translated onto greater or smaller scales. Some ghouls may want to run their cities. Others may be content with dominating individual people or sites.

Quixotism

This Derangement is the opposite of *Panzaism*. You believe everything you see or hear. Yes, there are faeries. That guy with all the hair, he's a werewolf. Oh, and by the way, this pendant came from Atlantis. You'll be out challenging windmills to personal combat before tea time, at least metaphorically. You probably came from a perfectly mundane background, and nothing out of the ordinary ever happened to you. However, now that you've been initiated into the secrets of the World of Darkness, logic has gone out the window. You are effectively down two Mental Traits whenever you are in a stressful situation.

Sadism

You resort to cruelty as a response when under pressure. Nothing relieves your stress like causing people pain. Physical pain isn't all you excel in, though. Sometimes mental anguish can last much, much longer. Whenever confronted with something that profoundly bothers you, you must either spend a Willpower Trait or find some way of taking out your anger on someone immediately.

Sycophancy

If there is one thing you know (and you know it well), it is that you cannot survive without your Regnant. She made you and she can unmake you. To keep her from leaving you to die, you do everything she says. In fact, you go beyond the letter of her law and do things that you think she would *like* you to do. If she likes classical music, get her tickets to the symphony. So what if they cost well over a hundred dollars. Isn't your life worth it? You spend your Influence Traits on frivolous things to make your Regnant happy, and thus find yourself caught short when crunch times come.

Revenant Character Creation

Specific guidelines for creating revenant ghoul characters can be found on page 65 of **Antagonists**. These are optional, and can be superceded by the basic ghoul creation guidlines in this book. **Note:** All revenant ghouls must pick a Path of Enlightenment at character creation beginning their in-game existence with a Path rating of 1. Revenants (with the exception of the Grimaldis) also have the option of learning Vicissitude as one of their Disciplines.

Chapter Four: Roleplaying and Storytelling

When we cannot act as we wish, we must act as we can.
— Terrence

Storyteller Incentive

There are several reasons for starting players off with mortal or ghoul characters (the rapid ghouling of mortals is perfectly acceptable in **Mind's Eye Theatre** games, and can be used as reward for new players who learn quickly). Setting up new players as ghouls instead of vampires reduces the overpopulation problem endemic to many **Masquerade** games. It's not uncommon to find 70 or more vampires in a city that's large enough to support perhaps one-tenth that number. By starting new characters as ghouls, Storytellers can maintain population balance.

Introducing ghouls also serves game balance. With new characters coming in as ghouls instead of vampires, the power level of the average character drops and gameplay is easier to manage.

Playing ghouls enables you to justify daylight events, and adds another layer to the intrigues of your game.

Starting players off as ghouls expands newcomers' roleplaying experience. They learn about the game even as their characters are educated by their Regnants.

Ultimately, playing a ghoul can lead to being Embraced. The precious nature of vampiric existence is emphasized by making players work for this "advancement." Who is more likely to appreciate the Embrace: a ghoul who's given long service in hopes of becoming immortal, or a neonate who was changed without explanation or cause? Furthermore, who will be better at roleplaying, the player who's developed a character toward a specific goal over the course of months of gameplay, or a newcomer who wanders into a game and is immediately made a vampire as a matter of course?

Player Incentive

This game is primarily about vampires. So why would anyone want to play a ghoul instead? There are several reasons.

Starting off as a ghoul is a perfectly acceptable way to get involved in any **Mind's Eye Theatre** game. This approach is ideal for inexperienced players; newcomers may not have had previous exposure to the World of Darkness. It's a lot easier to play someone who knows little of the true nature of things when one actually *doesn't* know what's going on. Starting an uneducated (in the ways of **The Masquerade**, at least) player with an uneducated character also helps to cut down information overload. Newcomers struggling to digest rules *and* background *and* history *and* character *and* the Traditions are likely to be confused. Having a Regnant there to teach her ghoul (while the Regnant's player helps out the ghoul's player) saves wear and tear on Narrators, and provides a more immediate source of information.

However, it's unlikely that "mere" ghoul characters will lack for things to do. Curious vampires will size up the potential threat of any and all

newcomers. So long as overzealous vampire characters don't regard all mortals as potential blood donors, ghoul characters will get the chance to do what they need to. In addition, ghouls have a few tricks of their own, and even a new ghoul may not be as overmatched by a vampire as one might think.

There are several things to keep in mind when playing a ghoul. A ghoul is a complex creature, inhuman enough to want to forget her past but human enough to fear for her future. Within each ghoul, Humanity and Beast engage in an endless struggle. The paradox is: The ghoul continues to exist only as long as the struggle within continues. Should Humanity triumph, existence as a blood drinker becomes unthinkable. Should the Beast win, little is left of the ghoul's original personality.

Every afternoon or evening, a ghoul wakes up knowing that she is excluded from both the mortal and immortal worlds. The only sanctuary she can find is with other ghouls, and even that comfort can be hollow. Still, the empathy of peers is the only refuge that ghouls can find. Understanding each other's suffering creates strong bonds between most ghouls, and they tend to look out for one another, especially those outside their own households. Competition for the Regnant's attention can arise within a household, over duties, and as a result of sheer proximity to people with whom you have little in common but your blood.

While ghouls are less powerful than their masters, sunlight is the great equalizer. A ghoul can almost forget the cold, undead hand that clutches at her heart when the sun warms her skin. But as the sun sets, her double life resumes. Of course, the vampire won't forget his ghoul's ability to walk the sunlit streets, and will certainly prepare a duty list.

Whether their Regnants are cruel or kind, all ghouls are enthralled to them to some degree. A vampire can symbolize everything a ghoul despised in life, yet she would still do nearly anything her Regnant wanted. How does it feel for a character to love everything she once hated? How would it feel for the most independent of individuals to need someone so desperately? This perverted devotion is unnatural, and most ghouls recognize that. However, almost all ghouls are helpless to act in the face of the Bond that ties (and gags) them.

Making the Decision

A player needs to be prepared to explore the uncharted emotional tragedy of the Blood Bond before she decides to play a ghoul. Playing a Bound character can demand that a ghoul act contrary to her best interests, out of the narcotic love that the Bond inspires. This love can make a character do things that she doesn't want to, things that she would never normally do, or things that are not necessarily in keeping with her long-term plans. To play a ghoul is to play a character with less than total free will, and players should think long and hard before accepting ghoulish restrictions.

Ghouls who interact with humans can feel a plethora of overwhelming feelings, from regret to anger to isolation. They can never let others, not even family or friends, know what is going on in their lives, though. Some break off relationships to avoid the pain or to spare loved ones the horror of discovery. The danger of a loved one witnessing a frenzy, the fear of a Regnant executing a friend as a "lesson" — these are the nightmares that haunt ghouls. Thus the majority of ghouls slowly but surely step away from their intimate human relationships. Ultimately, ghouls are more alone in a crowd than they are on their own.

On the other hand, the benefits intrinsic to being a ghoul can make such hell worthwhile. Many an Olympic medalist in the World of Darkness has ingested vampiric blood; it is the ultimate performance enhancer, and it can't be spotted in a drug test. Some vampires sponsor athletes, pitting them against the pawns of Kindred rivals in secret contests of one-upmanship. Sports stars, aspiring actors, musicians, politicians, lawyers and computer programmers have all benefited from the power of a Regnant.

Some ghouls even enjoy vampire politics, despite their status as supernatural second-class citizens. They find it easy to manipulate their Regnants after living with them so closely for so long. However, it is still a Herculean effort to gain any status as a ghoul in vampire society. Some ghouls offset their loneliness and rejection with the desire to be Embraced, to enter fully at least one of the worlds they inhabit. Others would rather die than lose all Humanity to the Beast.

Many vampires Embrace their most outstanding ghouls, as long as this change in status will not interfere with the ghouls' work. Other reasons for Embracing ghouls include rewarding servants for exceptional work, or moving trusted retainers into positions of more authority. Ghouls who are Embraced are often given more choice in the matter than are other potential childer. The transition from human to vampire is also less painful for a ghoul who has already seen vampire society at work.

Embraced ghouls retain the Disciplines they possessed as half-humans, but now their new clan Disciplines come to them more easily than they might have. Meanwhile, Disciplines not related to their new clans become as hard to gain as any out-of-clan powers.

The First Change

The change from mortal to ghoul is important to roleplay. The way the Regnant introduces her intended ghoul to the World of Darkness is crucial. Some vampires take a backhanded approach, tricking their intended Thralls into drinking the blood in a variety of ways. As soon as a victim of this sort of deception is Blood Bound and his new abilities manifest, the Regnant reveals what is really going on. These crucial tidbits are often dropped at a juncture that makes escape difficult or impossible, say, when the first vitae craving comes on.

Seduction is another means of drawing in a would-be ghoul, with the Blood Bond applied during the course of romance. When a Regnant reveals her true nature, a ghoul who has already been Bound is less likely to go into complete panic. The vampire's revelation to her new ghoul is a shock, of course, but the love he bears his Regnant no doubt provides him with the anchor needed to steady him at such a turbulent moment.

Of course there is always the heartless vampire who swoops down on an unsuspecting mortal and spirits her away to a cellar, where the victim is Blood Bound at the would-be Regnant's leisure. Such ghouls are more likely to rebel down the road; the trauma of their initiation into the World of Darkness taints even the love of the Bond.

All of these methods of exposing new ghouls to the supernatural have profound effects on their subjects. It is important to remember that before becoming a ghoul, a character's life might have been completely mundane. The sudden shift of reality can shatter beliefs, ideals and sanity. The challenge is in imagining how your character handles this rush of information. Think about it this way: she's just been offered eternal life and powers that no mortal can possess. In return, she has to agree to serve and protect her benefactor, who claims to be a vampire. All she has to do is drink this lunatic's possibly disease-infested blood….

Yes, presentation is very important.

Characterization in Play

When roleplaying, a player assumes the persona of her character. A character is going to change and be changed like a real person is. These can be simple behavioral alterations, the products of learning from experience, or changes can be as grandiose as the manifestations of new Disciplines.

Subtle changes occur, too; usually alterations of an emotional or mental sort. Betrayal is a good example. If a character is betrayed in the course of a game, she is probably more careful about whom she trusts in the future. Other characters may not understand this sudden change of heart (they may not even know about the betrayal), but the player does and doesn't necessarily need to explain.

People rarely understand what makes others tick, or what their reasons for actions are, and this should be reflected in-game. Just because a player knows out-of-game information about another character does not necessarily make that information her character's knowledge. The information is outside the game and therefore outside the character's sphere. If the prince is portrayed by a player's best friend, that doesn't make it right for the two unrelated characters to be chummy without a good in-game reason.

A Little Common Sense

If your character has irritated the prince and is dragged into court to be berated or punished, don't treat it like a joke. Remember that Kindred law is strict, most crimes are punishable by Final Death, and the prince is head honcho in a city full of unliving superpowered killers *for a reason*. More to the point, there's no reason for the prince to care if an annoying ghoul lives or dies. Playing a ghoul flippantly can lead to character death.

Just because you're playing a ghoul instead of a vampire doesn't mean the game is any less serious. Playing a ghoul is a license to step outside the strict rules of vampiric society, but don't abuse the opportunity. Invest your ghoul character some common sense, and don't feel that he's less valuable to the game than a vampire character is.

Experienced players don't need to play their characters according to stereotypes. Long-time players should look for challenges. If you normally stick to businesslike characters, creating an extrovert or artist might be a welcome change. If you're struggling to come up with something different (everybody's creative well runs dry at some point), another point of view can be helpful. Sometimes a Storyteller can offer suggestions based on the chronicle's needs, or a friend can play sounding board. If playing a ghoul sounds interesting, go to town. A player who normally creates brutes might find a cowardly Servitor fun, too. Those who typically play intellectual types might relish the opportunity to kick butt as part of a squad of Brujah ghoul roadies.

Storyteller Tips

Introducing ghoul characters might sound good, but how do these sorry creatures fit into a **Mind's Eye Theatre** game? Actually, they fit in pretty easily. Ghouls are great characters for all roleplayers, regardless of whether physical action or intrigue is important. Hunters, spies, bodyguards and chancellors — all of these roles and more can be filled by ghoul characters. Whether a ghoul slips into a vampire's haven for a little early morning spying, whispers plans into his Regnant's ear, or uses Potence to teach some manners to a snot-nosed neonate, he can be a force to be reckoned with.

Ghouls add depth to a game. They bring life to characters who, until now, were dismissed as two-dimensional henchmen. Elder vampires often have several ghouls who are never seen or played out, and all of these ghouls' actions ("I have my Servitors arrange the firebombing of that arrogant Tremere's house.") take place offstage, as exposition instead of action. With these rules, those faceless ghouls become flesh-and-blood characters, and have their own agendas (and allow important events like firebombing the Tremere to take place during gameplay).

However, it's important that ghoul characters aren't completely dependent on their Regnants. They should be able to partake of an evening's festivities even if their Regnants don't show up. If Michael plays Renee's Regnant, and Michael has to miss the game, Renee is put in an awkward position if she is dependent on their characters' interactions. However, if Renee's character is wrapped up in plots that don't involve her Regnant, she still has plenty to do while Michael misses all the fun.

Introducing ghouls who have player Regnants can be a challenge and a great responsibility for whomever plays the Regnant. This parental role is recommended for responsible roleplayers. That doesn't mean the Regnant is boring to play. The role simply demands maturity.

Storytellers might even want to encourage players to assume ghoul characters to help fill out their cities. After all, anyone can play a ghoul. Some might relish the challenge. Others might need convincing. Prod the reluctant along by suggesting that they create ghouls along the lines of the vampire characters they would have played. After all, they might get Embraced — if they're good.

Another technique you can use with ghouls is daylight play. This is one of the ghoul's greatest advantages. This is good for players who can't make an evening of it but who would still like to play. Players can be ghouls in the afternoon and Regnants in the evening. This sort of double casting takes a bit of planning, but is worth it.

Story Ideas

Ghouls can be used as plot hooks in storylines, drawing in vampires who have something to do with them, and even drawing in those who have nothing to do with them.

Hunters Hunted

Hunter ghouls have set up housekeeping in the city, seeking to stockpile blood and perhaps liberate a few brethren at the same time. To assist the used and abused, they gather vast amounts of information as payment from suitably grateful ghouls. This includes Influences, names of vampires' allies and enemies, access routes to havens, and details about vampires themselves. Such information can be used in a number of ways, from embarrassing abusive Regnants to sparking full-scale wars between vampires.

Hunters perform hostile takeovers of cities with nothing less than their lives at stake. Extensive sieges of metropolitan areas are time-consuming and dangerous, and the longer one of these operations takes the more the tide turns in favor of the truly immortal. Still, if everything falls just right, a cadre of Hunter ghouls can cut a swath of terror through a city's vampiric population before moving on to the next target.

When portrayed effectively, Hunters can throw vampires into full-scale panic. The thought of a Hunter prowling the streets in search of vampire blood may seem silly at first. The first kill ends the laughter, though, and sends

security bills skyrocketing. Even the most recalcitrant Brujah suddenly finds new appreciation for the Masquerade, which should be top priority anyway. If the Masquerade is broken frequently in your game, Hunters can be used to discourage vampires' antics.

Tales From the Crypt

Revenants are recommended for a different kind of horror. They can be introduced in a number of ways. The dilapidated old mansion that a Malkavian moves into already has residents: the Bratoviches. A Zantosa brings a date (a vampire's loved one or a favorite ghoul) home for dinner, and guess what's on the menu? The Tremere find they have competition in searching for a grimoire; the Obertuses are looking for the same book. A Ventrue prince learns that one of his trusted ghouls is actually a Grimaldi infiltrator, but which ghoul is it? And if there are revenants around, can the Sabbat be far behind?

Storyteller Note

Revenants bring plenty of disturbing qualities to your game, but a surfeit of weirdness can leave players numb. Be careful how you introduce such elements; give players time to absorb before showing them greater horrors. Too much strangeness at one time might leave them saying, "A horse with its stomach ripped out left on the mayor's front lawn? How gauche!" If you want to inject the occasional random act of violence (particularly in the case of revenants), add some kind of implied thought process to the scene. Dead people and animals are scary, but the line into terror is crossed when all of their organs are neatly laid out next to the butchered bodies. Suddenly the violence is no longer random; whoever committed the heinous act had a specific motive — a frightfully warped one.

Try to avoid the overused clichés of horror, such as pentagrams and the like. Familiarity breeds boredom. Always take plenty of time and use lots of detail to describe a setting or event that involves revenants. They are meant to be alien, and shouldn't be taken lightly.

You Rang?

Servitors, though basically the least troublesome of ghouls, are not usually prepared for the eternity that stretches out before them. More than one has been known to go insane from the crushing weight of years and the agony of the Embrace denied. Although this is possible with any ghoul, these unfortunates are very often attached to vampires of high standing, have the most responsibilities in a given household, and have free rein over a Regnant's Influences. Needless to say, these ghouls can cause a lot of trouble when they go rogue. Such ghouls are put down eventually, but hopefully with a measure of dignity, respect or sorrow.

Mood for this type of story can be anything from manic to somber. The poor ghoul was once perfectly normal and sane, perhaps even happy with her life. Encourage the Regnant to create memories of happier times, or other players to recall memories of interacting with the ghoul during her lucid days. Such recollections can only intensify the frustration and heartbreak of the situation, making the inevitable that much more painful.

Obsessive Servitors can spice up a game considerably. Ghouls who are driven by the false love of the Bond can become jealous of their household fellows or even other vampires. Nothing is as messy as an all-out war between ghouls, with their Regnant as the prize. Nothing is as dangerous as an obsessed Thrall who stalks his Regnant's companions.

Kindred Opinions of Ghouls

We often despise what is most useful to us.
— Aesop, *The Hart and the Hunter*

Everybody has an opinion on ghouls. Whether they hate them or love them, few vampires are truly neutral when it comes to these quasi-immortals. Members of the Camarilla view them as both a threat and a vital resource, inevitably falling back on the old cliché: "Can't live with them, can't live without them." Sabbat vampires take a dim view of ghouls. The unaligned clans have their own agendas for them.

Camarilla Opinions About Ghouls

Brujah

Old and wise Brujah make wide use of ghouls. Brujah prefer ghouls who are intelligent or reflexive rebels, and don't often plan beyond the act of ghouling itself. They may also ghoul human members of their gangs, but with the understanding that these people have proved themselves capable of running with the pack. Such people are also candidates for the Embrace.

Sometimes Brujah make ghouls out of sheer laziness. The vampires become tired of continually veiling their words or speaking in double *entendre*, and ghoul their human companions to allow themselves to talk more freely.

Gangrel

Gangrel think ghouls have as much right to true immortality as vampires do, occasionally more so. Ghouls are the responsibility of the Regnants who create them, since ghouls are practically childer. Gangrel don't create ghouls very often, preferring to take responsibility only for themselves; one, with a number of ghouls in tow are usually active in city politics. Gangrel are most likely to make ghoul animals; their command of *Animalism* ensures a tight Bond with their beloved pets.

Malkavians

Malkavians have no formal uses for ghouls, but prefer their helpers to be somewhat off-balance. If a Kook's ghoul of choice is not slightly insane at first, the Malkavian rectifies that as quickly as possible. Malkavians seem to like ghouls but don't keep many of them, finding them a bother to keep track of. When a Malkavian does take a ghoul, he uses the resource to the fullest. Crazy doesn't mean inefficient.

A Malkavian's Derangement is the key factor in how he treats his "toys." Those ghouls unfortunate enough to be chosen by extremely unstable vampires often have short life spans.

Nosferatu

These vampires have a hard time keeping ghouls until they are Blood Bound, and make use of *Mask of 1000 Faces* until they are. Most mortals just can't get past appearances.

Nosferatu don't need human ghouls as much as the other clans do, but they use the ones they have extensively (there are secrets that not even the Nosferatu can learn without the aid of normal-looking pawns). Animal ghouls are often created as bodyguards, haven defenders and messengers. They are also less likely to judge their masters by appearances.

The notorious Nosferatu spawning pools embody the heights of animal ghoul making. Within these burbling cauldrons of foulness, sewer creatures batten on Nosferatu blood and mutate into the most efficient home security systems imaginable. Few intruding vampires, no matter how thoroughly they may think they have done their research, are prepared for the monstrosities that a spawning pool can vomit forth.

Nosferatu prize a certain profile among their human ghouls: detail-oriented people who have inquisitive minds and aggressive attitudes.

Toreador

Toreador are infamous for picking ghouls for aesthetic as opposed to strategic reasons — living artwork to keep around the haven. Looks aren't everything, though, even for the Toreador. Poseurs seeking secretaries, chauffeurs or any sort of "help" deliberately choose those who look plain or dowdy, but who can get the job done. Servants should not outshine their masters, after all. Artistes are more likely to need housekeepers or assistants who can keep havens from falling apart, and who won't touch the works in progress in the basement.

Toreador as masters are a very mixed bag. Some disdain their ghouls as mere hired help. Others are protective employers. A few are imperiously cruel. They do, however, speak quite highly (even if it is with a surfeit of snide comments) of the joys of having Blood Bound ghouls to take care of things. For the most part this entails all the worldly duties normally taken care of in daylight hours (legalities, bills, banking, paying off parking tickets) that Toreador don't like to be bothered with.

Tremere

When they can get them, old-fashioned Tremere prefer illiterate ghouls who are incapable of reading their precious grimoires. However, illiterates who are competent at the tasks set them aren't easy to find.

Some Tremere select promising occult students for grunt work (especially work involving new Internet search vehicles and computerized library catalogs). They Blood Bond these agents as quickly as possible and liberally employ Dominate to ensure their loyalty. All Tremere who wish to create ghouls must have the permission of the local Regent, and must provide full dossiers on their would-be victims. Ghouls who are created without either are not tolerated. The offending Tremere is punished, and the unfortunate ghouls are executed.

Ventrue

Of all Camarilla vampires, the Ventrue are the most fond of ghouls. Some have 10 or more at any given time. Ventrue choose their servants based on what they need to control. How well a potential ghoul takes orders is important as well. Some Ventrue jokingly compare the process of choosing a ghoul to that of an employer picking among job applicants. Ventrue tend to treat their ghouls very well, but are careful not to let them grow too close. Ghouls are employees in Ventrue eyes, which goes a long way in preventing obsessive Regnant-Thrall relationships. Ventrue do, however, give more respect (and other rewards) to the highest achievers in their ghoulish broods, which can lead to fierce competition between ghouls. This competition has been known to turn deadly.

Sabbat Opinions on Ghouls

Sabbat vampires believe that ghouls are a waste of vitae and are good for nothing, not even cannon fodder. Ironically, few Sabbat strategists have seized upon the deep-seated discontent among Camarilla ghouls as a tactical advantage to be exploited. Sabbat hatred for Camarilla Kindred and for ghouls in general seems to blind the vampires to the usefulness of ghouls as weapons.

Those few ghouls within the Sabbat who are not part of the revenant families walk dangerously thin lines. A Sabbat ghoul can be destroyed for the most minor of infractions by any sect member, and the ghoul's "owner" isn't likely to argue.

Revenants themselves are barely tolerated. Only the political and spiritual weight of Clan Tzimisce shields them from total annihilation. The sect has already purged four of the revenant families, and many believe that a second purge is coming.

Antitribu keep ghouls, but consider them disposable when the agents' errands are completed.

Lasombra

Lasombra despise ghouls. If their Tzimisce allies did not support the little annoyances so emphatically, the entire subspecies would have been culled from the sect long ago. Lasombra ghouls are few and far between, and are kept mainly for two reasons: financial or political expertise, or skill at personal grooming. The former is self-explanatory; the Lasombra aren't fools and won't discard useful tools. The latter is explicable in light of the clan weakness. These ghouls serve as surrogate mirrors for their Regnants.

Tzimisce

The Fiends have more uses for ghouls than they can shape fingers to count them on. Of course, most Tzimisce ghouls aren't the happiest of servants, as their masters disfigure them until interaction with the mortal world becomes impossible. Tzimisce have even developed new varieties of ghouls, into which they installed specific emotions and personalities.

Szlachta are kept as guardians. They are so worked over with Vicissitude (bone carapaces, horns, callused skin) that they have lost all semblance of humanity, both physically and mentally. A vast majority have also lost the weakest grip on reality.

War ghouls, called *vozhd*, are the most rare of the Tzimisce creations. They are composed of several ghouls who are grafted together. *Vozhd* are most often used as siege weapons. Ghouls melded into one of these abominations lose their minds and Humanity in one fell swoop, and no one has found a way to restore them.

Some creative Tzimisce craft ghouls into furniture or ornaments for their havens. Still others have mastered the ability of weaving the hapless creatures into fashionable clothing (which, rumor has it, stays warm, even in the winter).

The revenant families were first created by the Tzimisce, and are sometimes used, even in their debased modern state, to breed promising candidates for future childer.

Neutral Clan Opinions on Ghouls

These vampires are more accepting of ghouls than are the Sabbat, but depend on them less than Camarilla vampires do. Members of the nonaligned clans often have surprising uses for their ghouls, and even more surprising ways of keeping them in line.

Assamites

All Assamites spend seven years as ghouls before being Embraced into the clan, so every Assamite has an intrinsic understanding of the ghoul's station. This may not cause an Assassin to spare a ghoul who gets in his way, but at least he won't despise the ghoul for what he is.

The Assamites choose their ghouls with an eye on the future. An Assassin's ghoul is not a servant. He is a potential Assamite whose worth is assessed throughout his half-human apprenticeship. Assamite ghouls are held to the same high standards as their masters are, specifically in regard to honor, truthfulness and dignity. Non-Semitic men (not to mention women) have only recently been selected as ghouls by members of this clan.

Caitiff

The clanless vampires keep ghouls as a survival mechanism. Ghouls provide backup whenever something big comes down. When intent on making ghouls, Caitiff seek out people like themselves: outcasts, misfits, the homeless and anyone else who might prove useful. These ghouls are usually drawn from the pools of mortals that the other clans have already surveyed, so the pickings get pretty slim. Beggars can't be choosers.

Giovanni

Giovanni ghoul those promising individuals who are not in the family, but whose expertise they wish to use. Power brokers, scholars, morticians, financiers — these are all good candidates for being "adopted" into the family. Members of the family who, for whatever reason, are not chosen for the Embrace may be sustained as ghouls for years.

The Necromancers have as many ghouls as the Ventrue do and utilize them in similar ways, but also use a few unfortunates as subjects in their studies. Any mortal who makes headway in the mysteries of the afterlife or who shows talent in spirit communication should expect an offer she can't refuse.

Ravnos

The average Ravnos values freedom so highly that enslaving ghouls is almost anathema. However, Ravnos create ghouls on rare occasions, and most of these are mortals with the mysterious Numina powers. A Ravnos typically chooses a mortal of Gypsy blood, specifically selecting a Rom who displays talents in the vampire's lost Numina. When a Ravnos drinks the blood of ghouls whose talents echo what his once were, he regains his powers briefly. (The only blood that can spark such a restoration of power comes from ghouls who possesses the same gift that the vampire had.)

Apart from this sort of special case, Ravnos shun the creation of ghouls, unless they can avoid Bonding them. Ghouls who do become attached to Ravnos should be wary of their masters' activities, lest a heist gone wrong leave them holding the bag before a very annoyed prince.

Setites

When a Setite wants a ghoul, she gets a ghoul, even if it's one already Bound to someone else. The Serpents have incredibly addictive blood and make good use of it, poaching ghouls from other vampires with ease. The Setite gives a taste of his blood to ghouls already Bound to other vampires. The original Regnants have no idea that their ghouls have been compromised, or that Setites are monitoring their activities through spies. Setites rarely keep human ghouls in their temples or havens, but do have a predilection for ghouling poisonous snakes. Cobras are particular favorites, though they are difficult to come by.

Anarchs

Anarchs keep ghouls much like Caitiff do, choosing their Thralls from roadies and loyal toughs. Anarch ghouls are often picked for their prowess at moving things quickly, by day or night. Nothing is more valuable to these vampires than the ability to get out town after the inevitable Blood Hunt has been called. There are times when waiting for nightfall to move would prove fatal.

AUNTIE CSILLA'S ADVICE FOR THE BLOODLORN

Dear Csilla,

I've been a reader for years, ever since I was made a ghoul. I was wondering if you have any advice for a Bound ghoul whose Regnant is mistreating him horribly?

Signed,

Miserable and Loving It

Dear Miserable,

We all know how grumpy Kindred can get, but it's not an excuse to beat on an innocent ghoul. There are Regnants out there who think they have nothing better to do than take out their aggressions on their Thralls. Some of them even do it for fun!

Sick of it? Sick of her pals kicking you around? Mispronouncing your name? Feeding on you without permission? Well, I'll tell you what, honey, there are ways of getting back at those jerks. And I'm going to lay out how....

But before I start, don't even think about saying "But mine's not like that." Uh-huh. If she weren't like that, you wouldn't be reading this column, dearie. If you get offended and put this down now, you're not a ghoul — you're a vampire in a warm suit.

Okay, it goes like this, kiddies: If you think revenge is a dish best served cold, huh-unh — it can be served hot. (Or you can make them think that, but that's my best and easiest one, and I should save it for last.)

Let me give you a little example I cooked up for my friend Armand. His kind, loving, generous Regnant decided to try him out as a bulletproof vest. In case you were wondering, it didn't go terribly well. He nearly died, with six neat little puncture wounds in him.

At any rate, my friend the pincushion hired me to get back at his Regnant, and this is the trifle I came up with to make her regret treating him that way. I call it Machka's Little Ditty. Don't ask about the name; I don't want to get Machka in trouble. She's working on her third Regnant now — the first two never knew what hit them.

Anyway, we're getting off topic. First, you need a sponge and a bit of paraffin wax. Water down the sponge, then squeeze it tight. You probably have *Potence*, so go to town. While the sponge is as scrunched up as you can make it, dip it into the wax and then freeze the little blob.

Then things get tricky. To use the Little Ditty, you need to get into your target's haven. This is no problem if you're doing it for one of the resident ghouls or for yourself, but if you're poaching a Regnant, watch out. Hopefully you know where your target's sleeping and what defenses she employs. If her ghouls are on your side, they won't be a problem.

On the way over to the mark, make sure you pick the wax off the sponge. Keep the bundle of joy in your hand so that it warms up a bit. When the time comes, you'll need it moderately well thawed.

Okay, now for the really dangerous part. You have a 50-50 chance of getting caught at this point, so be ready to run with *Celerity* at full tilt. As carefully as you can, toss the sponge down your target's gullet. If you can get it past the little dangly things at the back of her throat, you're in business.

Now comes the most important part — *run*. If you aren't fast, you're going to die. Hopefully you planned an escape route, preferably one that leads past bright, sunny windows. If the bloodsucker is in a high-rise, head for a corner stairwell and slide down the banister.

What is the result of this endeavor, besides leaving untidy wax droppings for anyone with *Psychometry* to discover? What can you possibly hope to accomplish? It's really sweet. The sponge thaws in the vampire's throat, where it expands and is irretrievable. In and of itself, that's just annoying. The funny part comes in when she tries to feed. Blood gets soaked up by the sponge so it can't nourish her, yet she can taste it back there. It's so tantalizing it hurts.

Once the blood congeals, things get really bothersome. What with this hard scratchy thing in her throat, your Regnant is going to break down or get help and rip it out the hard way.

Ever seen a vampire tear out her own throat? It's a treat.

Dear Csilla,

You've obviously been doing this for decades. What was the first trick you ever pulled, and which ones are your favorites?

Curious in Houston

Dear Curious,

I came up with my first trick with a Ravnos ghoul who I met at a truck stop on the way to Phoenix. She was fun, but her Regnant was too protective and bored me.

To be honest, it wasn't much of a prank. I just opened her coffin and nailed her feet to the bottom, then got in the car and drove like hell.

Of course, I've gotten much better since then. If you're about to change employment and don't really wish your old Regnant harm, use epoxy and stick something amusing to her fangs. Rabbit teeth work well, and have a high amusement value. Since vampires don't drool, this operation is surprisingly easy.

There are others that I'm fond of. A good one involves burning something in the haven. When your Regnant finally gets around to inhaling, he gets a lungful of soot and a faceful of panic.

I know childish ghouls who've thrown out all of their Regnants' clothes and then vamoosed, but that lacks flair. Naked or not, an angry vampire can still kill you. On the other hand, anything that can force a vampire to appear in court before sunset is good. The bloodsuckers usually get out of it, but it's fun to see them sweat blood when that summons for 10:00 A.M. arrives in the mail.

Dear Csilla,

My Regnant is a Ventrue, but he's not very good at business. He keeps losing business deals, and when he screws up he takes it out on me. I'm sure that if I worked harder he'd be more successful, but it's so hard with him abusing me the way he does. What should I do?

Your faithful reader,

Hopeless in Seattle

Dear Hopeless,

You're being too hard on yourself. Sounds to me like your Regnant is going to be some Lasombra's snack before long. You'd be doing yourself a favor if you moved on before it happened.

If you're really mad, stake the bastard and yank his fangs. You'll have no choice but to leave him. If you don't I think you'll end up dead sooner or later, anyway. Get going. Leave him to his fate. You have nothing to do with his screwups.

Dear Csilla,

I need something really special for my Regnant. He forgot the anniversary of my ghouling, and I'm kind of upset. I don't want to hurt him, I just want to make him apologize. Any suggestions?

Anxiously awaiting guidance,
Halfway Jilted

Dear Half,

You don't mind if I call you Half, do you? In any case, my best trick has got to be the Suntan/Sunburn routine. It's quick and easy. All you need is a beautiful summer day, some suntan lotion for yourself and a sunburn mask for the vamp in question. Go out and get yourself a nice dark tan. Don't worry if you burn a bit; that gives the prank the extra touch of verisimilitude that it needs. Come home before dusk and apply the sunburn mask to your mark. When you're finished, his pretty little immortal face will appear nice and burned. When he wakes up and sees himself in the mirror (unless he's a Keeper, but in that case you have bigger problems), he'll be at a loss for how he caught some rays. Did you take him to the park?

Of course, if he has no sense of humor, you're in trouble. In that case, my circulation drops by one. That's why I demand prepaid subscriptions, kiddies.

That's it for this week. I'm sorry I can't relate much more, but I have my Regnant's significant other to tar and feather. I might just cut off some of his hair while he sleeps and give it to a local Tremere. After all, it'll grow back before he comes to in the evening, and he'll never notice it's gone until the moment the first pin goes into the voodoo doll. Send those cards and letters with suggestions!

Take care, and remember: The only good Regnant is a humble Regnant.

CSILLA

Relations with the World of Darkness

Vampires are not the only creatures that a ghoul has to worry about. There are Lupines, mages and other Awakened beings who might not be friendly to a vampire in training. Not many supernatural beings have dealings with ghouls, unless contending with a Thrall's Regnant. Yet there's always that first time, and a ghoul should be prepared. Ghouls have also been known to cultivate secret relationships with Lupines friends whom they knew before tasting vampire blood. Ghouls have also been haunted by the wraiths of those they've killed in their Regnants' names.

Lupines

Few ghouls look forward to coming face to face with werewolves. Ironically, Lupines are the Awakened creatures that ghouls have to deal with most often. Ghouls usually radiate some Wyrm-taint to Lupines, and are considered to be little better than the Leeches they serve. Every so often an enterprising vampire experiments with making Lupine Kinfolk into ghouls. It usually backfires — badly. The victims' extended families attempt to slay the new ghouls as acts of mercy. Kinfolk ghouls who hope to survive better run far from their people.

Very few Lupines are made into ghouls. Most werewolves have violent allergic reactions to the Wyrm-taint in vampiric blood (assuming one sits still long enough to have some forced down her throat), and expel it immediately.

Perhaps one Lupines in a hundred can be ghouled, and these are regarded as one step short of Abominations.

Ghouls usually avoid werewolves whenever they can. As Awakened creatures, ghouls are not subject to the Delirium, and can see nine-foot-tall furry engines of destruction coming in plenty of time to get the hell out of the way. Some ghouls do cut deals with Lupines, but such exchanges are fraught with peril for both sides.

The Changing Breeds

Lupines aren't the only shapeshifters in the world, although they are the most numerous. Most of the other Changing Breeds have even less tolerance for ghouls than werewolves do. Mokolé, in particular, have nothing but contempt for ghouls, though this perception is perhaps skewed due to the sort of ghouls who go tromping around Mokolé lairs. Most of those unlucky Servitors are in the company of land developers who have their eye on a region. It's not surprising that the Mokolé have come to despise them.

Perhaps the most benevolent attitude toward ghouls is that held by the Nuwisha, who see them as means to get vampires' goats. A Nuwisha typically uses a ghoul to humiliate her Regnant, as opposed to killing the vampire outright.

Mages

Mages don't have many dealings with ghouls unless the Tremere are involved. Tremere often try to capture mages for study, sometimes turning them into ghouls in an attempt to extend their shelf lives. While this has the benefit of Bonding a ghouled mage so that he won't try anything tricky with Correspondence and sunlight inside the haven, the process can imperil a mage's Avatar and hence his ability to work magick. Ghouled mages who can no longer work wonders are generally pumped for information and then discarded.

Consors and ghouls in the same city often establish a *sub rosa* network, trading information and favors to make their respective masters happy. This underground servant connection can be a formidable force, and its members look after their own.

Wraiths

Ghouls have definite problems with wraiths. As ghouls are often called upon to commit dirty deeds for their vampiric masters, they can rack up sizable body counts. Furthermore, vampires tend to acquire large ghostly entourages. If a ghoul can become friendly with a wraith, the ghost can be a valuable source of information. However, most wraiths are unfriendly and inclined to cause ghouls trouble.

Risen

Risen are ghosts who have climbed back into their bodies to finish business on Earth. To come back, wraiths have to make deals with their Shadows. As part of a deal, a Risen might have to kill anyone it encounters, ghouls included. Risen also possess the ghostly ability Lifesight, so ghouls can't hide from them. Risen with less destructive Passions sometimes benefit from relations with ghouls, but these alliances are fragile and short-lived.

Risen can pass for vampires, and some seek out ghouls to help authenticate their disguises. An urban legend holds that an abused ghoul took advantage of her friendship with a Risen to convince her Regnant to straighten up and fly right. More likely, a ghoul would use a Risen friend to escape an intolerable Bond.

Changelings

Changelings generally avoid creatures as banal as the average vampire, but have an easier time with ghouls. It has been theorized that supernatural revelations make ghoul minds more flexible and capable of accepting oddities like the fae. Yet even childlings know that the apple doesn't fall far from the tree, and don't trust ghouls. A lucky ghoul may be able to cultivate a friendship with a fae, but the changeling is probably Unseelie and possesses an unhealthy curiosity about vampires. Seelie fae usually avoid ghouls entirely. Still, some look on these half-humans with pity.

Appendix: Animal Ghouls

You treat me like a dog,
Give me a bone to chew,
Frothing at the mouth,
Frothing all over you
— The Damned, "Rabid"

THE PET SEMINARY

Let's say you're a bright young vampire, but not a particularly wealthy one. You want a loyal ghoul, but without all the emotional baggage (and bills) that a mortal can bring. You don't want to hear all the insipid questions. You want to be able to say, "Frog!" and have your ghouls hop without asking, "How high?" Don't get yourself a human; find an animal that suits your needs.

Personally, my favorite species for ghouling is the dog. Borzoi, in particular, work well. They aren't as bright as other canines, but they are the most loyal and, without a doubt, the most capable hunters that you could ask for. But I shouldn't bore you by telling you how wonderful my puppies are when your needs might be met by other species.

A companion of mine, one with an impressive command of Auspex, keeps birds of all sorts for a wide variety of duties. While most adept at spying, birds are also excellent "silent alarms" and messengers for delivering warnings that most people can never trace. They are also fearsome defenders. You laugh at the thought of a "killer attack parrot," but a beak in the eye is nothing to sneer at. Multiply that by a flock of 20 and you begin to understand what my dear friend Niccolo sees in his little canaries.

Of course, Animalism is a prerequisite if you want to keep animals of any kind under your control. Vampires who seek to create animal ghouls without this Discipline find themselves in the same positions as the parents of teenagers: they have no way to communicate. Furthermore, vampire blood can make an animal very aggressive. The Beast in the blood seems to throw domestics back to nature, as it were, and even the most affectionate of pets become somewhat atavistic when they get a taste of vitae.

Most find the domestic canine best suited to life as a ghoul, but wolves are another story. Wolves are so... primal... that to attempt to enslave them with the Blood Bond courts disaster if you don't do it right. You have to consider their habits, the ways they challenge for rights of leadership — their whole societal structure. Domestic dogs, on the other hand, while they do revert to a more natural state, have human concepts ingrained into their skulls. This makes them open to life with, and dependent upon, a true master. You become pack leader, the alpha.

No matter what type of animal you ghoul, you have to deal with its degree of domestication. Some culture is better than none. Otherwise the poor beast may never develop any kind of intelligence. For example, my eldest dog Doran is capable of reasoning, and the occasional bit of deductive logic. Though he's not terribly good at it yet, he can still make better decisions than just about any animal on Earth (at least, any animal that's been around for fewer than five centuries). Mind you, Doran isn't much brighter than a six year old, but he's improving. A few more decades, and he'll be brighter than my Congressman.

I find that most ghoul animals get brighter, but it is a slow process. Borzoi are not the clearest thinkers, nor are Dobermans or greyhounds. Their thought processes can take centuries to improve. On the other hand, while primates have intellects that mature rapidly, they are almost uncontrollable when ghouled. It has something to do with the way the Beast warps them, I think. I won't give my blood to a monkey (marmoset, gibbon or any other primate, for that matter) again after the last experiment I conducted. The property damage was in the tens of thousands of dollars, not to mention the injuries inflicted on my person.

Useful animals include the ferret, which is excellent for thievery because it can get into air ducts and other tight spaces. Horses are less useful than they used to be (we have cars now, and mounted combat is passé), but as far as I'm concerned, they still rank ahead of felines. Damned cats never do anything, and they expect you to feed them whenever they want, which is usually at the least convenient times. Rodents work well for information gathering; no building is rat-proof. (If you want to extend the principle and give your blood to cockroaches, you're not likely to get much useful information back. Insects are simply unintelligible, and ghouling them is a waste of blood.) Goats are still popular with one clan. The Ravnos insist on their utility, but I have no idea what they're talking about. Nosferatu are fond of giving blood to alligators for obvious reasons. However, keeping alligators requires sewer access or a suitable pond, and a lot of spare corpses. It's not like you can stick one in the bathtub and hope it will stay.

Of course, your choice of ghoul species is dependent on your whereabouts and clan affiliation. A Nosferatu has more use for an alligator than she does a goat (unless she's hungry). A Ravnos might find a gator on a leash to be awkward. Consider your situation, then figure out what sort of creature works best for you. And if you're still skeptical about the whole notion, remember this: An animal ghoul never asks for a raise.

Stella di Riganoni
Proprietress,
The Pet Seminary

Rules for Creating Animal Ghouls

Animal ghouls are highly regarded in vampire society, often more so than human ones. This is due in equal parts to their unquestioning loyalty and their inability to complain. While animals do have certain drawbacks (it's hard to get one to change a zoning ordinance), they are unsurpassed in their skills as sentries, spies and personal guards. However, animals aren't as intelligent as humans; players should not choose animal ghouls as characters.

Animal ghouls can be used for protection in a haven, and as agents for gathering intelligence. However, keep in mind that ghouled animals can be easy to recognize. Most vampires will become suspicious of oddly curious animals that hang around too much. With that in mind, be prepared to lose an animal that your character brings to an evening's event.

Logistics

To simulate an animal ghoul at your side, make up a card that lists the animal's Traits and wear the card prominently when the creature is with you. Stuffed animals can be used to represent small ghouls (although a teddy bear may cause you to be mistaken for a Malkavian). Even these should have stats pinned to them to indicate their status as ghouls, not toys.

If you send your ghoul on a mission, inform a Narrator of the action and hand her your ghoul's card. She can assess the difficulty of the task, decide what tests your ghoul has to pass, and determine what tests others have to make to impede your ghoul's progress. The card should be returned to you when the mission is completed, unless the ghoul doesn't come back.

For example, Bertram sends his ghouled pigeon off to spy on his rival, Ernest, so Bertram's player talks to a Narrator. He explains what he wants the pigeon to do, then hands the Narrator the ghoul's card. The Narrator finds Ernest's player and asks him to make a Static Mental Challenge. He succeeds, so the Narrator rules that Ernest notices the pigeon. Ernest knows the pigeon is Bertram's, but isn't worried about it and does nothing. The next time the Narrator sees Bertram's player, he returns the card and provides rudimentary information on what the pigeon saw.

Narrators shouldn't drop everything to run ghoul missions — animals aren't likely to take the shortest route between two points, and may not do things in a hurry.

Common Sense

A note to players: Do not bring your pets to an event, even if your character has a ghouled pack of combat-trained Great Dane-schnauzer crossbreeds. It's too dangerous for the players and your pet. And no, we're not even going to mention the problems that a lack of facilities might create.

Animal Ghoul: (3-5 Trait Merit)

This Merit may be purchased after gameplay begins (but the ghouling of the animal must be roleplayed). The would-be Regnant must possess intermediate *Animalism*. Otherwise the ghouled animal won't follow commands and will go rogue.

A 3-Trait ghoul would be a bat, cat, small bird or rodent. A 5-Trait ghoul would be a large dog (German shepherd, Irish wolfhound) or one of the bigger cats (leopard, cougar). Vampires who attempt to ghoul exotic species also have to deal with the associated baggage: the care and feeding of large predators in between doses of blood, providing enough space for the animals, permits, and protests from animal-rights activists. There's more to ghouling a leopard, feeding it the occasional Blood Trait and announcing a *fait accompli*.

Creation

A ghoul should be created according to the rules presented here, and based on the animal Trait descriptions on page 158 of **The Masquerade: Second Edition**. The player adds a number of Traits to the animal's description equal to his character's rating in the Merit: *Animal Ghoul*, minus one. These Traits should be reasonable; gerbils with *Brawny* x 3 are right out. Next, the Storyteller selects one appropriate basic "physical" Discipline for the ghoul (e.g., *Potence*).

Every ghoul animal also has a Trait called *Instincts*. This Trait relates to the animal's natural tendency to rebel against orders given to it. A wild animal has a base Instincts Trait of 8, while a domesticated animal has an Instincts Trait of 5. Rather than take extra Traits for a ghoul, a player can buy down its Instincts Trait at character creation by one level for each Trait sacrificed. After ghoul creation, the experience cost is two points to reduce one level of Instincts.

Instincts comes into play whenever a character attempts to command his ghoul. A Static Social Challenge is performed against the *Instincts* Trait. *Leadership* or *Animal Ken* Abilities may be used to re-test this challenge.

A ghouled animal immediately acquires the Negative Trait: *Violent*. Any wild animal (use common sense; wolves are wild, dogs aren't) also has the Derangement: *Crimson Rage*.

Uses and Abuses

An animal ghoul may be used in a variety of ways. A Gangrel with a wolf ghoul might use it as an ally in combat. In this case, mob-scene rules come into effect, and the wolf loans a Physical Trait to its master. A Toreador with a bat for a ghoul might use it to spy on her rivals and watch over her while she sleeps; the Storyteller should arrange a Static Mental Challenge for the bat against an opponent's defenses. The possibilities are endless. However, if a Storyteller feels that these rules throw the game out of balance, she should limit or eliminate the use of ghouled animals.

Example of Animal Ghouling

Dan's character, a Toreador Poseur named Octavius, has just attained the intermediate level of *Animalism*. He decides to spend three experience points and takes the Merit: *Animal Ghoul*. He settles on ghouling a vampire bat, after talking it over with the Storyteller. Dan figures the bat will go nicely with Octavius' Goth image. The Storyteller is amused by the possibilities and potential logistic problems.

Dan and the Storyteller discuss the matter, and agree that acquisition occurs through the use of Octavius' second level of basic *Animalism*, *The Beckoning*. However, as Dan's chronicle is set in Kansas City and vampire bats are creatures of the tropics, Dan's character has to spend an appropriate Influence to get into the local zoo after closing, and gain access to the vampire bat exhibit.

In the next session, the Storyteller and Dan meet again. The Storyteller announces that Dan's attempt to acquire a bat as a ghoul is successful. Now it's time to assign extra Traits.

Dan decides to give his bat the extra Trait *Dexterous*. He also decides to buy down his bat's Instincts Trait to 7. As the ghouled bat is only a 3-Trait Merit, this takes care of the extra Traits that the bat can acquire.

Dan has no choice but to give the creature the Negative Trait: *Violent*. Since this is a naturally wild animal, he also has to give it the Derangement: *Crimson Rage*.

Now that creation is complete, Dan names his bat Evil and hands the animal's rough character sheet over to the Storyteller. She decides that *Celerity* is the best Discipline for a bat to have. A note is made of this, and Evil's stats are transcribed onto a large card which Dan has to wear whenever Evil accompanies Octavius.

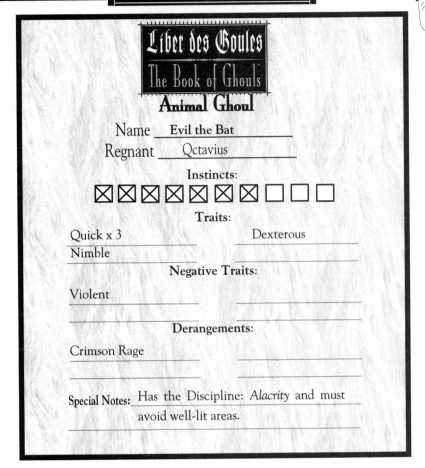

Liber des Goules
The Book of Ghouls
Animal Ghoul

Name ___Evil the Bat___

Regnant ___Octavius___

Instincts:

☒☒☒☒☒☒☒☐☐☐

Traits:

Quick x 3   Dexterous

Nimble

Negative Traits:

Violent

Derangements:

Crimson Rage

Special Notes: Has the Discipline: *Alacrity* and must avoid well-lit areas.

Animal Ghouls and Experience

A character may spend her own experience points to buy her animal ghoul Disciplines, and to buy down the ghoul's Instincts Trait. She cannot buy it Abilities, Influences, Attributes or the like except by special arrangement with the Storyteller.

To buy an animal ghoul a Discipline, a character spends the amount of experience that he would normally need to learn an out-of-clan Discipline. This translates into four points for basic Disciplines and eight points for intermediate. No animal ghoul may ever possess advanced Disciplines.

Buying down an animal ghoul's Instincts rating costs two points per Instincts Trait.

Liber des Goules
The Book of Ghouls™

Animal Ghoul

Name _____

Regnant _____

Instincts:

☐ ☐ ☐ ☐ ☐ ☐ ☐ ☐ ☐ ☐

Traits:

_____   _____

_____

Negative Traits:

_____   _____

_____

Derangements:

_____   _____

_____

Special Notes: _____

_____

Status

Backgrounds

Disciplines

Abilities

Negative Traits

Mental Traits

Social Traits

Physical Traits

Merits   Flaws

Humanity

Willpower

Blood

Influences

Derangements

Liber des Goules
The Book of Ghouls

Player_____

Character_____

Chronicle_____

Nature_____

Demeanor_____

Concept_____

Regnant_____

Regnant's Clan_____

Haven_____

Experience_____

HOW THE WEST WAS WON!

IGNORANCE

OF THE

LAW

IS NO

EXCUSE

Laws of the Night
The pocket edition
of the rules for **Masquerade**.
Now Available

Laws of the Hunt
The pocket edition
of the rules for **Apocalypse**.
Summer 1997

OBLIVION

live action for the dea